Reiki & Reiki Meditation: The Comprehensive Guide

Heal Yourself and Others, Restore Balance and Create Unlimited Abundance

By Marta Tuchowska

www.holisticwellnessproject.com

2

Contents

General Overview of Reiki 16

Chapter 1: Cracking the Reiki Code and Making It Your
Lifestyle 20

Chapter 2: Understanding the Healing Essence of Reiki and
Letting it Work for Your Highest Good 37

Chapter 3: Reiki as a Holistic Therapy – The Limitless
Possibilities and Benefits of Reiki and How It Can Change Your
Life and Help You Become a Better Person 46

Chapter 4: Reiki and the Subtle Energy - How Reiki Actually
Works and How You Can Make It Work for You and Your
Loved Ones 58

Chapter 5: Explore Your Chakras, Realize Your Weak Points
and Balance Yourself with Reiki. Simple Healing Techniques
You Wish You Had Known Years Ago! 69

Chapter 6: Reiki and Its Amazing, Powerful Exercises for
Wellness, Health, and Abundance–the Practical ABC's! 85

Chapter 7: Reiki Symbols and How to Use Them to Let Go of
Past Situations, Create an Incredible Future and Attract
Abundance 92

Chapter 8: Common Questions and Misconceptions about Reiki
Explained 99

Conclusion: Embrace Reiki and Feel Amazing Like You Have
Always Wanted! 107

Introduction

What's one of the biggest problems that modern, 21st century people are facing? Stress. I am sure you know and understand this issue. I also know that you are interested in natural therapies and healing. You realize that the real healing and peace come from getting to the root of the problem, rather than masking the symptoms. I really feel like congratulating you for taking your first steps in exploring a fully natural and revitalizing healing system called Reiki. I am sure you will love it. Even if you feel sceptical now (I used to be extremely sceptical at first and now I regret it), I am sure you will give it a chance and enjoy its holistic healing benefits.

The best part is that you can do it on yourself and others (even on animals and plants)! I will show you step-by-step how to connect back to the Universal Energy and use it to restore balance and health–not only physical, but also mental and emotional. As you already know, it's all interconnected. An unhealthy body can result in unbalanced emotions and an unfocused mind just like mental and emotional stress can lead to diseases that manifest themselves on a physical level.

After reading this book, you will basically have two choices:

1. Keep applying what you have learned from me in order to work with your energy, feel it and practice self-awareness. This book will expand your horizons when it comes to meditation, healing and spirituality–with more tools, you will become more creative with your own holistic self-care practices. Whether you are new to chakras, or are chakra-obsessed, like me, I will invite you to join me on a journey

of self-discovery that will result in creating happiness, health, and abundance.

2. Take it to the next level by becoming a Reiki I practitioner and finding a local Reiki master who will guide you through the process of Reiki attunement. This is a really important decision and this guide is also designed to help you prepare yourself and make the most of this life-changing experience. In case you already are a Reiki practitioner, I hope you will find this book refreshing and will use it as a reference for yourself and your clients (or as some people prefer to call them- patients).

I welcome you all my friends! I believe everyone can learn something from the following pages. What I am just about to share with you has been inside me since I was a kid. I always felt like there was some kind of a Universal energy and bond.

I would always feel sad when seeing people fight– something deep inside me was telling me that it should not be that way. The more that people walk away from the universal healing light, the more harm they do to themselves and the more difficult it will be to get back to the roots–being connected with Universal love that protects us all.

I am a very sensitive and sympathetic person. Whenever I would see someone suffer, I would ask myself why and what I can do to help them. I always felt the energies around me–some people call it female intuition, but I think it's more than that. I think it's your decision to form a part of this incredible world and your willingness to take small but important actions to make this world a better place.

The answers to my questions came when I discovered Reiki, actually in my very late twenties (a few months before turning 30 actually). You know the feeling when you are told to do a math exercise, and you try to do it intuitively and you miss something in the middle and you ultimately fail. You think: *Man, if there was something like a rule, I could do it better!* In other words, you know that there must be something, like a template, a rule, something that helps you classify and organize your knowledge.

Well, my friend, Reiki is similar. If you are a sensitive human being asking yourself questions, I am sure that deep inside you, you already know what your conscious mind is just about to read, absorb and apply. To be honest, I think it's something that all human beings knew when they are born.

Unfortunately, as we grow, the fast-paced society takes away our intuition and natural healing skills. This is why we might need a rule, a template to stick to, in order to solve an equation of life....

Who am I and why I wrote this book?

My name is Marta, and I am 32 years old (as of 2015) and my mission is to help you create a balanced and healthy lifestyle full of happiness and abundance. I am really passionate about wellness, natural therapies, personal development and spirituality. I love combining all of my knowledge as well as personal experiences (and even struggles) to empower modern and busy individuals to create a stronger version of themselves.

I am a certified massage therapist, wellness coach and Reiki 2nd level practitioner. My journey of self-discovery has led me to Spain, where I studied a bunch of natural healing therapies like lymphatic drainage, naturopathy, nutrition, macrobiotic diet, alkaline diet, aromatherapy and even beauty and spa techniques. I am also currently studying NLP (Neuro-Linguistic Programming).

As you can tell, I like the holistic approach, and I know you will agree with me: one cannot deal with the body, mind and spirit separately and expect vibrant health and personal success. One needs to commit themselves to constant personal development and working on their body, mind and spirit at the same time. The results? By taking this approach, you will be able to improve all areas of your life, increase your intuition, and simply know where you're going.

This is why I love Reiki and other alike natural therapies. However, when it comes to Reiki, it's easy to learn. Everyone can do it. It is much easier than, for example, dominating complex natural medicine systems like acupuncture or acupressure.

Reiki is even easier than massage. All that you need to master it is intention. You don't need to learn any complicated movements like is the case in deep tissue massage, and you don't need to study human anatomy. Let's leave the anatomy work to doctors and physiotherapists.

As a side note, more and more hospitals are combining conventional medicine with Reiki treatments, as the latter helps patients feel better, and it helps to create a positive mind-set. If you really want it, you will learn it fast, and you will be able to practise it on yourself and others. You will reap a better quality of life!

Back to anatomy- we will be diving into what I call: deep, spiritual anatomy and there will be 7 major chakras to learn and feel. Reiki is more about feeling and experiencing than about knowing and having some kind of information on your "hard drive." So, no worries, don't focus on details, but on the bigger picture. I really want you to relax as you are reading the following pages.

Have you ever had this feeling, that even though you are healthy (for example you eat healthy and you exercise regularly), and your doctor is proud of your self-care, you actually don't feel that healthy? It's simple. You are not connected. You lack healing energy. Some of your chakras

may be imbalanced. The good news is that with Reiki, you can easily get back on track and really feel GOOD and HAPPY! Reiki is one of the most marvellous and effective chakra balancers and you can do it everywhere and anytime.

I still can't believe I am writing this book. Even a few years ago I would laugh at Reiki and similar energy working therapies. I was really sceptical. It wasn't until I fully experienced its healing and soothing effects that I fell in love with it, and I made a decision to become a Reiki practitioner myself (and so can you if you want to).

You see, in the last few years, I have made some really significant changes in my life. The turning point in my life was when I found out I had uveitis, which is a really rare eye disease (it can even result in blindness).

I realized that even though I thought I was relatively healthy, I actually wasn't. I lacked balance. I did not feel fulfilment, something was missing. Prior to my disease, I already had interest in natural therapies, and I was actually studying massage therapy. I quit a stressful office job, and I invested all of my little savings into education. I wanted to change my career. While in the process of achieving my professional goals, uveitis struck me out of nowhere.

At first, I felt very sad, but then I realized that everything happens for a reason. A Universe, a God, whatever you feel like calling this governing force above us, very often sends us signals so that we can finally move in the right direction.

What I learned was that I needed to recover balance. I have lived many years with stress (even though I did not realize it), and I felt lost. I spent most of my early and late twenties partying and working in jobs I hated just to make a living. I felt trapped. I was far away from my true vocation. At the same time, as a sensitive person, I would question this "system." While trapped in it, I could neither create nor

contribute. As a result, my emotional wellness was gone. I thought that the best anti-stress therapy was to go for drinks with "friends," followed by a nightclub and very often an after party.

By the way, most of those friends turned out not to be real friends, especially when there were no drinks and parties from my side anymore. Still, people are on different stages of their journey and do things in their own way. I don't want to preach to anyone. I wish them well. Everything happens for a reason...

My disease made me come up with a simple conclusion: all imbalances accumulate in your body for many years. You may think you are healthy, or you believe you are, as people tell you so (because they see you munching an apple here and there). Before my disease, I already had plenty of information on holistic self-care.

I even got started on Reiki...

However, to know is one thing and to apply is another. You see, I had this information in my head, but not in my heart. As soon as you have it in your heart, you intuitively apply it when you need it.

Sometimes we really need to "cut off our heads" (not literally of course) and use our hearts more.

This is my message to you: don't repeat my mistakes. Sometimes, less information is better, as long as you apply it and practise it. For example, you might pick up only one technique or inspirational piece of advice from this book and apply it and benefit from it almost immediately.

Simple example of information vs. inspiration: as a massage lover, I love getting massage treatments done. When looking for a massage therapist, I don't really care how many years they have been practising and how many certifications they have accumulated. Obviously, I don't want anyone inexperienced working on me, but I also care about other factors.

I remember getting a treatment by someone with 30 years of experience in many therapies, including acupressure and reflexology, along with Chinese Medicine. Then, I also got a treatment done by a massage student who had only just started on simple relaxation massage training, but for some reason, her treatment worked better for me.

She only knew a few strokes and that was it, yet it helped me. I believe this is because she was focused and had the intention of helping me, whereas the first therapist seemed to feel a bit tired and burnt out (not good! Reiki surely could help).

It's all about using your heart. We tend to intellectualize too much sometimes.

Okay, I know that some of you may be getting bored... You might be thinking, "The author talks too much about herself!" But you need to understand that in order to be successful (no matter what it is that you want to achieve), you need not only information, but also motivation and inspiration. The last two are conveyed by personal experiences. It's simple, as most people relate better to other people and real-life situations.

There are plenty of books on Reiki. I am not saying that mine is better than others, it's not my point.

What I am saying is that the essence of all Reiki books (including mine) is pretty much the same. The information is always the same (or similar). Some books may be more advanced, some shorter, some of them may only have 20 pages...This is information. However, the same information changes depending on its teacher. Everyone is different. This is the beauty of life!

One of my new empowering beliefs is that there is always something to learn from everybody (even though, at first glance you might not resonate with them).

It all comes down to opening your heart and letting your intellectual mind go on a well-deserved vacation.

Let's repeat again: we need information, motivation and inspiration.

What did Marta do wrong a few years ago? She had plenty of information but lacked motivation and inspiration. You see, I am not a perfect guru. I am like you, a seeker. A dedicated seeker. I seek wellness, holistic wellness for others and myself. That's my mission.

This is why Marta understands what it really takes to be successful and she wants to help you avoid unnecessary failures.

Okay, I need to stop talking about myself in 3rd person. It is my intention that this book provides you with detailed information on Reiki and satisfies your intellectual mind (we need to feed it with information).

But I also hope that my occasional stories and personal experiences that I throw in here and there (in moderate amounts, so as not to bore you) will fuel your heart with inspiration and motivation, as well as passion.

Introduction

I do not include personal stories to brag or to feed my ego. I use them to illustrate the information that I provide in the following pages of this book. I have the feeling you will like them. My mission is to make holistic lifestyle design easy and fun. I want to make it practical.

In this book, I also include pictures so that you can get started on self-healing as soon as possible. It's me in the pictures, so you will know who's talking to you. I don't have a fancy studio/expensive camera, or anything like that and so I just use simple pictures I took from my phone (with a very deep intention of helping You on your journey). I am a big believer in being resourceful and moving forward (using the means that were already given to us). It's not about being perfect. This book is not perfect. I am not perfect. But I know what my intention is. Whatever it is that you do, start with your why!

Back to uveitis, the eye disease I mentioned before. I managed to heal myself. I found an amazing ophthalmologist named Marivi who is also a homeopath and TCM (Traditional Chinese Medicine) practitioner. I used homeopathy and balanced nutrition backed up with a mindset (as my ophthalmologist used to say: *this is a war and we have to keep fighting!*), as well as Reiki meditation.

I would be up early in the morning every day and do Reiki self-healing meditation. It helped me achieve a positive mindset that I believe is the key to health success (or any other success), especially when you struggle with disease.

I am not a doctor. I cannot make any claims. I wish I could. But I can't. I can only spread the word of Reiki and encourage people to practise it alongside other natural therapies and balanced lifestyles.

Now, it's time to dive into Reiki.

Take in a few deep breaths. Burn an incense stick or use aromatherapy essential oils in a vaporizer. Play some gentle music in the background. Let's enjoy the journey of holistic personal development....

FREE MINDFUL EXPLORATION NEWSLETTER

Before we dive into Reiki, I would like to invite you to join my Mindfulness Email Newsletter so that we can stay in touch.

As soon as you sign up, you will receive a free bonus audiobook from me + other inspiring tips and techniques to help you on Your journey.

You can sign up at no cost by visiting my private website at:

www.HolisticWellnessProject.com/mindfulness

If you happen to have any problems with your download, email us at: info@holisticwellnessproject.com

I can't wait to connect with You via email, and I hope you will enjoy my newsletters!

General Overview of Reiki

As you already know, more and more people are looking for natural healing and relaxation techniques that can make their lives free of stress, tension, and illnesses. One of the most popular healing methods is the Reiki System, which can provide you with an amazing effect not only in your body, but in your mind and spirit as well.

Reiki is a term used to represent the Universal Life Force Energy, which is said to be within and around all entities. To give a more precise idea of the word, *Rei* refers to the universal Divine Spirit while *ki* refers to the life energy. This life energy corresponds to that of "Chi" in acupuncture, "Prana" in Yogic traditions, and "light" in Christianity.

Dr. Mikao Usui

Dr. Mikao Usui founded the Reiki System. He was a Japanese Buddhist practitioner, who had an extensive background in a number of philosophies and religious teachings. On the other hand, although Reiki appears to be a spiritual practice (which can complement various medical methods and treatments) it is not a religion. The practice of Reiki does not have a specific doctrine. As such, irrespective of religion, faith, age, educational attainment, gender, or race, everyone can take part in a Reiki session without compromising religious beliefs or principles.

The primary purpose of the Reiki System during a session or treatment is to allow the highest good or the subtle energy to flow to the individual specifically in areas where he/she needs it most. Apart from alleviating the individual's body, mind, spirit, and emotions, Reiki can help relax, revitalize, and counterbalance his/her well-being.

Reiki can help you in the detoxification of the body, speed up the healing process, and treat certain types of illness. In the same way, it can also awaken your healing ability, release blockages in the energy field, enhance creativity, manifest goals, and heal relationships. Most of all, Reiki can help in aligning you with your Divine purpose. This is what Reiki did for me—it helped me reconnect with myself.

The Reiki System involves various techniques for channelling the subtle energy to a person through the hands into a subtle energy system. It regenerates vitality and energy balance through alleviating both the physical and emotional effects of suppressed stress and tension. Reiki is powerful! It gently nourishes and efficiently opens blocked chakras and meridians. It encourages healing and better health; thus, a person can feel at ease and relaxed.

The Reiki System is taught in a manner that is very unique from other healing methods. The Reiki Master transfers or channels the Reiki to his/her student during an attunement process. During this process, the crown, heart, and palm chakras of an individual are opened. These body parts are said to be the energy centers. Consequently, the attunement process is when the student, the Master, and the Spirit source create an interlaced special connection.

The Reiki process of attunement can be an efficacious spiritual experience for an individual. It is where the energies are channelled towards the student through laying on of hands as well as breathing on the crown chakra. This process increases a student's psychic sensitivity and awareness. Moreover, once a student receives the subtle energy, he/she will have it for the rest of his/her life.

During a Reiki healing session, the client, who is fully clothed, is asked to lie down on a massage table where an aura (more on auras later) or body scan will be carried out. This will discern the areas where the Reiki energy is most needed. The Reiki practitioner or healer will then place his/her hands above the body of the client while running them slowly from head to feet. The practitioner or healer is expected to follow a standard protocol for hand placement or may conduct the healing session through his/her intuition. Usually, a Reiki healing session may last from 1 to 2 hours. The session ends with an aura cleansing method where a client is asked to take fluids and continue doing so to ease the body and release toxins. The client will also be asked to do self-healing affirmations and meditations.

I personally know some people who don't like massage, as they just don't like the idea of being touched by someone they don't know. Reiki can be a great solution for them. They remain fully clothed, plus there is no direct touching involved, as a Reiki healer keeps his or her hands 1-2 inches above the client's body. The sensation is really nice. Even though there is no real touch, you may feel warmth or gentle tingling. There might be some nice memories that awaken in your mind (I always go back to happy childhood memories when someone is healing me with Reiki). In some cases, certain past traumas and bad experiences may be brought to light, but...it's only a part of the healing process. The sensations will tell you a lot about yourself, and you will know the answer that will guide you in your journey of self-discovery and self-improvement.

Receiving Reiki allows an individual to open his/her heart and mind. Reiki paves the way for an individual towards his/her true self. On the other hand, the path of Reiki is a practice that lasts a lifetime just like other paths for spiritual and personal growth. An individual who receives Reiki becomes a lifetime student who will discover continuously that what one needs lies within.

This was only some general, warm-up information. We are now going to discuss the most important Reiki and Reiki meditation concepts in detail...

Chapter 1: Cracking the Reiki Code and Making It Your Lifestyle

Reiki is a term referring to a healing and holistic self-development system. It is pronounced as "Ray-Key" or "LayKey" in Japanese. In the early part of the 20th century, Dr. Mikao Usui created the Reiki System in Japan. This system of healing and self-development is often referred to as Reiki Therapy or simply, Reiki.

It is now becoming popular in different terms including, "Usui Reiki Ryoho," "Usui Reiki Treatment," and "Usui Reiki Healing Method." In the Western part of the world, Reiki is known as Usui Shiki Ryoho or Usui-style Healing Treatment/Method. On the other hand, in some countries across the globe, Reiki Therapy is known as Usui Do, which refers to a philosophical or spiritual path; Usui Teate, which refers to hand-healing; and Usui Reiho, which refers to a spiritual method.

In general, Reiki Therapy is referred to as a synergistic integration of energy healing techniques, self-development practices, and spiritual healing. Although it is a system, which is highly influenced by therapeutic and spiritual ideals and discipline within Buddhism and Shinto, Reiki is not a religion or does not have any particular religious doctrine.

I think it is important to mention because I know many people who don't feel like giving Reiki a chance, as they believe this practice would be against religions they follow. They thus remain sceptical about Reiki, aura cleansing and chakra balancing practises. Remember, no matter what your religion is, Reiki respects it and is willing to help you embrace holistic wellness the way you deserve...

Reiki as a Generic Term

The word "Reiki" has received a generic status for the past few years. Some people refer to it as a hands-on practice, a high-level Chinese Chi Gung healing practice, or forms of Western spiritual healing. In other places, Reiki is cited as a method used to enact healing miracles of prominent religious figures including Jesus and Buddha.

I prefer to simplify things as much as possible. You see, life is already complicated enough. There are many ways to do the same thing and achieve exactly the same result. A hairdresser or a stylist may be using different products and techniques, yet they still create the same result and make their client's hair look amazing.

Reiki is no different. If you were to see the way I do Reiki (on myself and other people) and then compare it with other Reiki practitioners, you would surely see many differences in the way we do it (technically). However, the result would very often be the same. If I were to teach you exactly how I do it, you would also develop your own, intuitive style later down the road. That being said, you would do it differently, on a technical level.

The essence, however, always remains the same...It's about cultivating one's intuition and feelings. Let your inner spirit guide you. Use the information as a starter, not as a final destination...

A great number of people have confessed to taking the very core of Reiki Therapy to different cultural and spiritual practices and even belief systems after undergoing Reiki training. As such, many versions and new styles of Reiki have manifested through the years. Most of these may be referred to as Reiki-influenced or Reiki-derived systems of healing and personal development.

Reiki as an Energetic Radiance

Based on the original intention of Dr. Mikao Usui, Reiki is only a therapeutic and self-development system. The term indicates the amazing therapeutic phenomenon or energy radiance, which is found at the core of this natural healing system. *Rei* in the term Reiki is translated as "universal" or something that is sacred or spiritual. It can also mean "soul." *Ki*, on the other hand, is translated as "life force energy," or something that implies feelings or "spiritedness."

That being said, Reiki can be interpreted depending on an individuals' perspective. It can be a "life force energy," "universal," "spiritually-influenced life force energy," or a "charismatic healing radiance."

Reiki as a Gentle Therapy

Reiki is both profound and powerful, yet it is a gentle, non-invasive therapy. It helps reduce stress, provides relaxation, enhances the self-healing properties of the body, nurtures and replenishes vitality, and supports the immune system. It can be integrated to various medical practices and other healing therapies. Reiki is also a healing therapy that stimulates an individual's relaxation response.

Reiki is a truly holistic therapy. This means it acts mainly through drawing out a healing response in an individual's entire spectrum, which is physical, emotional, mental, and spiritual. Unlike other therapies that act only on a physical level, Reiki can aid in emotional issues as well as nurture a better sense of balance and wholeness in an individual's life. Reiki is also beneficial in treating certain physical disorders and nervous conditions while encouraging an improved well-being. Thus, Reiki as a gentle therapy indicates no negative side effects.

Now I really feel like taking a short break and "Reiki myself up!" For me, it is like a holistic cup of coffee! So, let's have a cup of Reiki coffee together, shall we? Be my guest!

The Principles/Concepts of Reiki

The Reiki System of healing and self-development is guided by a set of five principles, which are referred to as the *Gokai* in Japanese. These wonderful principles are central to the Reiki System specifically in assisting an individual to transform his/her attitude towards life, putting balance into one's self or soul, and responding with compassion, regardless of the situation.

These are very important- nobody is perfect, I always say we are all fragile human beings. I don't know about you, but I am far from being perfect, still, I go for progress in all areas of my life. You all can take action to improve your life straight way.

Simply take a piece of paper and a pen, and write down the following Reiki principles and read them aloud. Keep the list in your wallet, car, on your PC, in your office and in your vision board. It will help you in difficult moments. You will know what is right for you and those around you and you will find it easier to stick to it...

The Reiki Gokai (Five Principles) have various translations that are slightly different from each other; however, they all start with "Just for today" and end with "for the improvement of body and soul."

The Reiki Gokai includes:

Just for today...

(1) Do not succumb to worry

(2) Do not rise to anger

(3) Manifest compassion to all beings

(4) Apply yourself diligently

(5) Express gratitude for all of your blessings

These principles of Reiki intend to invite blessings as well as encourage the spiritual medicine to cure illnesses. Based on the principles of Reiki, these concepts should be applied every morning and evening while in a seated prayer position, repeating the words aloud and into the individual's heart. You can actually start applying it straight away. I find it really powerful. Make Reiki principles your affirmations. Once thing is certain: something will change in your life...

How to Become a Reiki Practitioner

The first requirement in order to be a Reiki practitioner is to go through a training, which is often structured in levels or degrees. An individual who wishes to learn and carry out Reiki goes through an "attunement" or initiation in which Reiki can be awakened or activated within him/her. The duration of the training may take from two to even seven days.

It all depends on your Reiki master. Mine was supposed to take three days. It was me and two other girls really fascinated about the topic. However, in this particular case, our Reiki Master decided to give us a couple of extra days of "training" (I think the word "training" does not sound too Reiki, but it also reflects how we perceive things in this world).

He believed we were already extremely prepared to receive Reiki and very sensitive and so he decided to equip us with extra tools, more deep attunements, chakra breathing meditations and guidance. We also practised our skills on one another. It was an unforgettable experience.

For now, don't get too obsessed about finding Reiki training (unless you have made this decision and found your Reiki master prior to reading this book).

I recommend you give yourself some time, and practise the exercises I will be showing you later on in order to feel your energy. Once you have started working on your healing energy, you will be more open to receiving a Reiki attunement from a Reiki master.

My suggestion is that for now, you should focus on yourself and try to get as much as you can on your own. Chances are that as you go deeper and deeper into a self-healing process, you will actually attract the Reiki initiation course (or Reiki attunement) without even looking for it. That was actually my case!

There are many Reiki masters with great energy and vocation and you should always follow your intuition when looking for someone who will guide you through the first level of Reiki.

Here, in Barcelona, Spain where I live, there are plenty of schools and therapists offering Reiki attunements. I remember that a few years ago I was looking for one for myself, and I would always get turned off for some reason or another. Or a given school seemed too "salesy" for me, and I did not feel like the attunement would be personalized enough for me. Or some of their therapists would seem to lack passion for what they were doing, and I just did not feel attracted to their training.

Now, since I don't want to be judgemental, I prefer to put it this way—they were Reiki schools, courses and therapists that were put there for a reason for sure, and wanted to change lives of other people. I found them on my journey, but it was still not my destination. However, they helped me realize the qualities of a Reiki Master I have always been looking for and finally found...This is why I encourage you to give yourself some time...

I found my Reiki master when I wasn't even looking for a Reiki course...He was actually sending out e-mails to his friends telling them about the upcoming Reiki courses he was preparing. And for some reason my e-mail was there in his contacts.

The best things happen when we don't spend more energy than we were supposed to and we actually find them. To tell you all the stories to back it up, I would need to write another volume (and I am sure I will if you are interested). Reiki and law of attraction go hand in hand. When you feel good (and Reiki makes you feel good), you CREATE a good life.

The Reiki attunement involves the channelling of the subtle energy from the Reiki Master (teacher) to the student. The Reiki Master recalibrates or re-patterns the student's subtle energy centers, as well as the etheric field.

The Reiki training for becoming a practitioner begins with Level 1 in which the attunement or initiation opens or introduces the student to the Reiki flow. In Usui Shiki Ryho, Level 1 emphasizes the hands-on therapy for self-treatment and treating others mostly at a physical level. This is the outer focus of Level 1. The inner focus, on the other hand, is learning to be "a clear channel" of Reiki.

In general, Level 1 involves learning the ability to "step out of the way" in order to let the Reiki phenomenon transpire. It is about prevailing over the desire of the individual's conscious mind that might impede in the healing process. It is about learning how to be detached from things, feelings, and events that might hinder in the flow of Reiki. Ultimately, Level 1 involves "letting go and letting the energy flow." After completing this level, there will be usually a 21 days body and soul detoxification period during which you will be asked to:

1. Practise Reiki on yourself every day (self-healing meditation, chakra cleansing and practising hands positions. We will get to these later in this book);

2. Eat a clean diet: avoid processed foods and animal products. I recommend sticking to a plant-based diet

during that period, however you are also asked to listen to your body and not be too strict on yourself; (if you are interested in plant-based, alkaline concepts, I highly recommend you join my free Alkaline Wellness newsletter for more resources:
www.HolisticWellnessProject.com/alkaline)

3. Try to be outside in nature as much as you can, or at least listen to the relaxing sounds of nature;

4. Let it go and be nice to others;

5. Extra suggestion (this is what my Reiki master advised me to do): start a journal and a dream journal. Write down your dreams and thoughts and use them as guidance. During my Reiki initiation process, I was told that my throat and third eye chakras were really open and that I am blessed with creativity.

    This is why I was encouraged to take it to a new level. I think it's thanks to this tip and exercises, which I was doing alongside other Reiki practises and personal development that I managed to unleash unlimited levels of internal motivation and creativity and began to write. I think it was dormant for many years…If it hadn't been for Reiki, I don't know if I would be here, writing this book for you, and hopefully inspiring you…

    After completing the 21 days of new Reiki habits as well as body and soul detoxification, you can start healing others. Here, I don't refer only to people. You can also apply Reiki on animals, plants, food and water. My cats love Reiki! They always come to me, when I do Reiki on myself and try to get as close to my hands as possible. I think they can feel the Universal energy! Cats are amazing!

Again, depending on your training and your spiritual teacher, you may be given different guidelines. I am talking from my own experience here.

Level 2 of the Reiki training involves intensifying the quality of the awareness of the Reiki flow as learned from Level 1. In Level 2, the student is presented with symbolic tools, which allows him/her to develop intentions as well as extend the scope of therapeutic healing.

Level 2 involves the introduction of the three sacred symbols to the students and it teaches to use them to carry out treatment at more intense psycho-emotional levels, enhance efficiency of physical level treatment, and perform remote or distant healing. With the symbols, you can even heal past situations (for example when you hurt someone or you got hurt).

You can also use symbols to go to the future situations, for example, you have a stressful job interview and you want to program your subconscious mind to make it stress-free and successful. You can even use the symbols to program your mind for abundance (it really helps you expand your mindset and change your relationship with money).

The great thing about Reiki is that when practised regularly it can help you connect with your real self so that you take a meaningful and purposeful action to ultimately do what you are meant to be doing.

There is nothing worse than knowing you are not headed in the right direction, but you know you lack guidance to be back on the right track. It's amazing what Reiki can do for you and how it can change your perspective.

Of course, always remember that you may not act from greed, and your actions must benefit yourself and others. You cannot utilize Reiki just to satisfy your financial hunger.

Some people visualize checks and wait for the unexpected to happen, but I believe that Reiki is designed to help you reach your full potential in your career, finances and business.

There are many opportunities out there and they are perfect for you, you simply don't realize they are there for you. Reiki can help you expand your mindset and increase self-awareness. I even know some corporations and CEO's who practise Reiki and organize corporate Reiki sessions so that they employees benefit from it as well and work happier, utilize their intellect, and stay more focused.

I will give you all the details about symbols later in the following chapters. For now, I just want to sketch a general picture of all different Reiki levels and what they teach you.

I remember that during the Reiki II course, a few really incredible events took place. Our Reiki master told us to do a simple exercise to try to heal a past trauma or any past even where we either got hurt or hurt someone. I remember there was a girl who came to our Reiki gathering feeling very sad.

Apparently, a few months earlier, she and her boyfriend of many years split up and there were many arguments, tears and suffering. This girl decided to apply the symbols and other techniques she had learned during the course. She wanted to go back to the past and at least try to heal what happened so that they could stay in touch as friends.

Now, during the Reiki course, we had to switch off our mobiles and all electronic devices.

So, we were given some time to send healing Reiki power to the past. I felt a bit sceptical at first, but I decided to let it go. It was a hot summer, the end of July. The climate in Barcelona is very humid and combined with hot temperatures it made me feel tired. Still, I decided to concentrate and try to think of any past situation I could actually try to heal. To be honest, I did not really believe I could, but with Reiki, it's not that much about believing, it's about allowing it to heal *you*. And so I did allow Reiki energy to heal a situation from the past.

Now, I could think of dozens of past situations to apply this technique, but at that time, I could not think of any, so I picked up the first one that came to my mind. When I was about fifteen years old, I had a really good friend; however, we were both gossiping and calling each other names behind the other's back, which ended up in tears from both sides. As a result, we never talked with each other ever since, aside from the short "hi." This friend actually left Poland (where we were originally from) when we were sixteen, as her mom decided to immigrate to North America. I never heard from her ever since. At that time, we did not have e-mails to communicate fast. Some other friends from school would keep in touch with her via letters, but it was short-term. Few teenagers would spend their free time writing letters to Canada, while they had other stuff to do. So I forgot about this friend for a while, but I think she was in my heart and I wished we could just make things good again.

Here is what happened:

I first did the exercise and felt a bit relieved. But I did not notice any extraordinary sensations. I just felt at peace with myself. I felt I could forgive and also receive apologies. Shortly after the exercise, we did a short meditation and then we decided to have a break and go outside to the near park. We also wanted to get more water (not only because of the summer heat, but also because of Reiki- you very often get this sensation you need more water to purify yourself, at least we did!)

My course companion, the girl I mentioned earlier, went to a nearby store with me and then we sat on the bench. She decided to switch on her mobile to check the messages, as at that time she was looking for a job and she wanted to see if there were any missed calls.

She suddenly looked very surprised and excited. I asked her if she got any good job offers. She said: "No, but it looks like my ex was calling me and he left 3 voice messages!" She felt a bit anxious to check them out, but I encouraged her to do so. I left her alone and told her to take her time and call him back if she could. She looked nervous but happy.

It turned out that they hadn't spoken for a few months. All of the sudden, he called her asking to apologize and see if there was a chance they could meet up and make things work again.

The break was over and I went back to the course. I told my Reiki master what happened. He did not feel surprised. He said that all of us were going to have a pretty amazing week, and he couldn't wait to hear about it. He told us to feel free to call him or e-mail him at any time. He was really passionate about teaching Reiki and his time always seemed unlimited.

To finish the story, my course companion and her ex boyfriend got back together and now 2 years later they are happily married and have a wonderful baby girl.

Of course, one can never use Reiki to manipulate emotions and relationships. Reiki will do what's right for you. If your former relationship was supposed to work, it will be brought to life again and the old misunderstandings will be cleared up. If, however, it was not right for you and the other person, Reiki will simply heal the past trauma so that you can move on. This is a really important principle. You cannot use Reiki to make someone fall in love with you or do something against their will, or something that is not good for them (or for you, even if you don't realize it). Reiki is free of emotional manipulation.

Three days after the course, I got a Facebook friend request from someone I did not have any friends in common with and at first glance could not recognize. It took me a few minutes to think, hold on, this is my old hometown friend!

Her name was still the same, but the surname was Americanized, so I could not recognize her at first. I accepted her invite and we reconnected. I asked her, how did you find me? She said, last weekend (exactly when I was doing my Reiki course) I was thinking about you and I decided to check if I could find you on Facebook or LinkedIn. I typed in "Marta Tuchowska", only hoping you did not get married and did not change your surname! I wasn't surprised to see you live abroad because I remember you were always good in languages and wanted to live in different countries.

Pretty amazing, right? It's nice to reconnect after 15 years, plus we have even scheduled to meet up on either side of the Atlantic at some point!

This is only a tip of one iceberg of what Reiki can do for you. Some people also call it the Law of Attraction. Call it the way you want, it will change your energy and your life. It will help you feel at peace and gradually eliminate past traumas, heal past situations, make you feel present in the here and now and prepared for an amazing future of self-growth and self-discovery.

To name similar stories, I would really need to come up with another volume...if you really want me to, please let me know in the review section of this book! I would love to hear from you. Maybe you have similar stories?

Finally, Level 3 of the Reiki training is referred to as the "Master" or "Teacher" level in which the student will already demonstrate his/her ability to channel the Reiki to others; thus, the student can now be referred to as a Reiki "practitioner." At this level, the practitioner develops a deeper connection with the Reiki flow.

A fourth sacred symbol, the Master symbol, is also introduced to the practitioner and he is taught about its uses and significance in the entire attunement process. Level 3 of Reiki is still something for which I am preparing myself. I will do it whenever it feels right for me. For now, I feel I still need to be more congruent with practising and feeling what I have learned so far.

Although most Reiki students choose to reach the highest level of the Reiki training, which is Level 3, some are perfectly fine with just reaching Level 1. This is because

Level 1 already provides the basic awareness necessary for practicing Reiki healing both for self-treatment and treating others.

A few more words (I think I have already mentioned it, but just in case, to re-enforce it):

Whenever working with Reiki, both on yourself and others, you don't utilize your own energy, but you use the infinite, healing energy that comes from the Universe.

If you are sceptical about Reiki, you may laugh, and I will allow you to do it. I used to be sceptical myself and would call it some "hippie dippie" stuff. But you see, sometimes it's not about the "WHY", but about the "HOW" that shows itself in tangible results we see, feel and even hear..."WHY" can be difficult to get, mostly because we are used to living in our dimension...but...

Finally, what is the difference between Reiki and Reiki Meditation?

Here is my definition: both are actually the same, they have the same essence which is healing with the Universal Energy connection. I usually refer to Reiki as a healing system, the essence, the substance and a tool. When you take this amazing tool and apply it to yourself in order to purify your energy field and restore balance or try to address any particular problem of physical, mental or emotional nature, you actually create your very own and precious Reiki Meditation.

My Reiki Meditation may be different than yours, because we are all different. However, the essence will be the same and so will be the healing energy.

Again, it's just my way of perceiving things. I believe that

Reiki is a form of deep, holistic meditation. If you are not new to meditation, you may enhance your existing practise with Reiki meditation. All you need to do is to start applying Reiki principles and other practical tools this book will teach you.

Chapter 2: Understanding the Healing Essence of Reiki and Letting it Work for Your Highest Good

Like I have briefly mentioned in the previous chapter, many versions of the history of Reiki have circulated in different parts of the world. Most of these versions are unverified and lack a factual basis. As such, some people who feel incomplete with the current versions are still undertaking the quest for the true roots of the Reiki System.

On the other hand, there is one version of the history of Reiki, which is considered the most accurate and credible. This version came from the combined testimonies of traditional Reiki Masters, early initiates of Mikao Usui, and members of the Usui Reiki Ryoho.

Traditional or Japanese Reiki

The Founder of the Reiki System – Mikao Usui

Mikao Usui was born on August 15, 1864 in Yago, Japan. He lived in pursuit of obtaining Spiritual Truth through his studies of Buddhism. His fascination for the Buddha's ability to heal brought him to create the Reiki System. He travelled to a giant cedar forest known as Mt. Kurama, which is outside Kyoto. There, he prayed and meditated at a Buddhist Temple that established by a priest known as Gantei. The temple was built in honour of Bishamon-ten, referred to as the Spirit of the Sun. Mikao Usui stayed in the temple for 21 days.

During his first day, he piled 21 stones. At dawn, he would toss one away to keep track of the length of days he stayed in the temple. On the last day, Usui looked to the horizon where he saw a beam of light shining towards him. According to Usui's first initiates, the light that their Sensei referred to had consciousness. It asked Usui his willingness to receive the healing information that the light offered. As Usui avowed his willingness to the light, the beam struck his forehead and knocked him unconscious.

Initiation

While Usui was unconscious, he saw colored bubbles of light with symbols inside of them. Usui meditated upon the bubbles and gained the knowledge of how to use the symbols for healing. That was Usui's initiation into using subtle energy for healing.

Not too long after, Usui discovered that the subtle energy can heal physically as well as emotionally. In addition, Usui discerned that the subtle energy balances the spirit and awakens the person's spiritual gifts as well. He discovered that the subtle energy aids in achieving happiness and inner peace.

I personally believe that we were born with this capacity to even spoil ourselves with incredible wellbeing; however, our fast-paced and very often materialistic society takes us move away from our real essence. One of the best healers is nature and I propose to you that you try to do as many of the Reiki and Reiki meditation exercises as possible that I will be showing you, outside in nature. You may find it way easier to connect, because you will be in the real, natural environment that you were supposed to live in.

What you can also do right now, as you read this book is to take a break and put it down!

Pre-Reiki exercises that will help you feel more focused and connected:

Sit comfortably the way that feels right for you. Take a few deep breaths. In through your nose, and out through your mouth. Imagine the white and purple light entering the top of your head. The light is warm and healing. It enters your body through your head and travels down to all your cells and organs. It gives you the energy you need. Let the light be present. Let the universal wisdom enlighten you. For now, forget about unpaid bills and taxes you need to file. It will get done and you will do it all right once you have felt good like you deserve. You need to slow down for at least five minutes a day. Even the busiest person can do it. Instead of having a coffee break, you can have a self-healing break!

This is a really simple yet effective pre-Reiki exercise. You can even do it when you can't sleep. Imagine that the light relaxes you, all of your muscles: physical, mental and emotional. You can do it while commuting to work. If you work with people and you know that some of them absorb too much of your energy and leave you drained, you can also use this technique.

Simply focus on the white and purple healing lights entering your head as you talk to them. You can also imagine the same lights entering their heads. Simply let the intention do it for their highest good. Most people are mean or not nice, because they are hurt, sad or unhealthy. They need your help, and you can help them with these simple, "pre-Reiki" techniques. I will show you how to cleanse yourself as well as your working and living spaces from negative energies that some people may be spreading (either consciously or unconsciously) later in chapter 4.

By doing the white-purple light pre-Reiki exercise, you will feel the so-called subtle energy. This energy is something that cannot be clearly defined, but can be clearly felt. You probably know what I am talking about. Imagine you have a date, and you really want to be with that person, but you can feel that there is no reciprocation. Or, you enter a room full of people and you can feel that there is someone staring at you, you turn around and you confirm it's true. These examples are nothing else but different contexts of subtle energy.

Developing and Teaching Reiki

After going through his own initiation of the subtle energy and discerning the benefits of this healing energy, Mikao Usui created the Reiki System along with a healing clinic and society in Tokyo. He started giving Reiki treatments in April, 1921. He also taught Reiki classes in his organization known as Usui Reiki Ryoho Gakkei.

Usui created his Reiki System and taught it based on three levels or degrees. The first level is Shoden, which means the first teaching. The second level is Okuden, which means inner teaching. The third level is Shinpiden, which means mystery teaching. Apart from the three levels, Usui also developed the Reiki Attunement ritual (usually combined with the first level of Reiki training). A Master uses this ritual to initiate or commence a student into the subtle energy.

When an earthquake struck Tokyo in September 1923, Usui took his Reiki System into the city and treated the survivors. From there, the word spread all over Japan about his healing ability. Usui then travelled throughout Japan and provided help to people whenever he could. For the rest of his life, Usui spent his days healing people. He died from stroke on March 9, 1926 in Fukayama, Japan.

Basic Philosophy and Lineages of the Reiki System

When Mikao Usui conducted his Reiki classes and sessions, he did not ask for a mandatory fee. In fact, he sometimes gave treatments to his patients and students free of charge. Usui's philosophy was to teach Reiki based on the principles of the Meiji Emperor. Usui meditated upon these principles that we have already mentioned in the previous chapter:

(1) Do not get angry today

(2) Do not worry today

(3) Be grateful today

(4) Work hard today

(5) Be kind today

You can re-phrase it as:

Just for today, I am free from anger. I am free from worry. I am humble, I am honest. I am compassionate about myself and others. Repeat this a few times sitting in a prayer position.

Feel free to create your own Reiki prayer.

In addition, Usui taught that any individual has the ability to access Reiki because it is found within oneself. Before Usui died, he was able to give the Master Teacher Attunement to sixteen of his students. Most of them taught and created their own Reiki systems based on Usui's principles. One of the students was Dr. Chuujuru Hayashi, who was responsible for the spread of the Reiki System in

Western countries.

Reiki's True Home

The true home of the Reiki System remains in Japan to this day. Although some Reiki organizations specifically in the West created titles such as "Lineage Bearer" and "Grandmaster," there is no such title in the Japanese or Traditional Reiki. The titles were only created in reference to the structure of the Reiki organization.

Reiki in the Western World

Mrs. Hawayo Takata is the person who brought the Reiki System to the Western world. Takata was born in Hawaii, USA, but her parents were both Japanese. In 1935, Takata visited Japan to seek cure for her illness. She chanced upon a Doctor Chujiro Hayashi, a retired naval officer who was practicing Reiki. In 1937, having been treated from her illness through Reiki, Takata returned to Hawaii where she established her own Reiki practice.

Takata received her certification as a Master of the Usui Reiki System in 1938 from Dr. Hayashi. She was also authorized to teach Reiki to other people. In the early 1970s, Takata went to mainland America and introduced her Reiki system, which is known as the Usui Shiki Ryoho or Usui Style Healing Method. In just a short period, Takata's healing art of Reiki became extremely popular as many people who sought treatment were relieved and cured. Some also sought to learn the Reiki for themselves. In 1976, Takata granted certification to her first Reiki master, Virginia Samdahl, who was part of the 22 students also to receive certification.

Before the death of Takata in 1980, she taught her students that for an individual to become a "Reiki Master," he/she has to teach at least one class apart from receiving Master Level attunement. Takata said that in order to become a Reiki master, one has to teach and attune to at least one student.

Takata's version of Reiki soon spread through word of mouth. However, some people who participated in Reiki sessions found something missing in the art. Thus, they went to Japan and rediscovered the original Reiki founded by Misao Usui.

Here is what you have learned about Reiki so far (you can start applying straight away)

- Subtle energy- if you haven't done it, I urge you to do this simple pre-Reiki exercise right now;

- Reiki is a simple holistic healing system designed for the masses: everyone can do it;

- Reiki is about having good intentions. Observe those around you. Don't judge them, but sympathize with them and practise forgiveness. Think about what you can contribute to the world and how you can help others- just like Usui did;

- Make the 5 Reiki Principles the core Principles of your holistic lifestyle and use them in your prayers;

- There are many kinds and schools of Reiki, because different students have different styles and they pass their knowledge to their students, rather than thinking judgementally about which approach is right or better. Embrace the fact that everyone is different. Each and every Reiki practitioner who wants to help spread the word of

Reiki is unique. This is a beautiful life. Everyone is different. These differences form the foundation of holistic medicine of which Reiki is a part of.

Chapter 3: Reiki as a Holistic Therapy – The Limitless Possibilities and Benefits of Reiki and How It Can Change Your Life and Help You Become a Better Person

Reiki is considered as one of the most versatile healing systems, given that it can be integrated with other healing and medical practices. It heals not only on the physical level, but also on the emotional, mental, and spiritual levels. As mentioned in the previous chapters, Reiki works through the subtle energy that balances the mind, body, and spirit.

With the advent of different holistic therapies today, Reiki remains one that emphasizes solely on the body's energy. It maintains that the body is stronger and the mind and emotions are balanced when the life force is flowing abundantly and freely.

A Reiki healer is able to analyze patterns between his patient's imbalances. Certain symptoms on physical levels go together with other mental and emotional problems and the other way round. Like any holistic health practitioner, a Reiki healer wants to get to the root of the problem (for example some major chakra imbalances) and restore balance, wellness, and happiness.

There are many benefits of Reiki specifically as a holistic therapy. Some of its most prominent benefits include:

(1) Providing tranquillity and balance in mind, body, and emotions

(2) Providing relief to many physical ailments and pain

(3) Being applicable to people of all ages

(4) Preventing future ailments

(5) Aligning and balancing the chakras

Providing Tranquility and Balance

Today, more than ever, the responsibilities that people have to face every day can be very taxing. As life gets doubly hectic and stressful, most people tend to drain their life force energy while their minds become unfocused. When you are stressed or pressured by various situations in life, your tendency is to develop negative thoughts and feelings resulting in mood swings and difficulty in interacting with others.

Reiki can aid in bringing back the mind and emotions into a balanced state. This is something that we all need, don't we? Reiki can be a great and natural way to enhance your relationships, communicate better and very often just forget about the past, forgive others, ask them to forgive you and simply let it go.

Through regular Reiki treatments or sessions, you can be back in focus and unify the dispelled energies. Reiki allows you to release negative emotions, improve memory, and have clarity of mind. All of these result in reducing stress and fatigue; thus, you will be able to think clearly and make better decisions specifically to fulfil YOUR goals and achieve inner peace and happiness.

Without stress, the immune system will also be enhanced. And we all understand that having a strong immune system means vibrant health and unstoppable energy.

Again, this is the best natural coffee for the soul!

Providing Relief or Cure to Many Physical Ailments

Apart from the mental and emotional benefits that Reiki provides, it can also provide relief to many ailments of the physical body. Reiki enhances your life force energy, which runs throughout your body. This brings balance to your organ systems and boosts your immune system to encourage healing, instead of reducing symptoms.

Some of the health conditions that can be relieved or cured through regular Reiki therapy include: migraines, asthma, sciatica, insomnia, chronic fatigue, arthritis, and menopausal symptoms. In addition, Reiki can also aid in the faster recovery for an individual who has undergone surgery.

The best part about Reiki in terms of curing physical ailments is that it can be integrated with other healing methods and medical practices. It does not have any adverse effects on the ailing individual. Remember that I am not a medical doctor or a therapist and I am not making any medical claims.

However, if you are undergoing any medical treatment, these can be combined with Reiki. Remember not to disrupt any medical care or medication intake without consulting your doctor first. Do not reject standard medicine, for you will always need regular check-ups with your doctor as well as possible tests and diagnoses. Remember how I told you about my experience of curing uveitis? I was in hands of an experienced ophthalmologist, I followed all her guidelines, and I utilized Reiki as an extra tool.

More amazing benefits and facts about Reiki that will leave

you no choice, but to practise it...

Applicable to People of All Ages

Anybody, regardless of age, can receive Reiki treatment for physical, emotional, or mental problems. Babies, toddlers, young children, teenagers, adults, and the elderly can all experience the benefits of Reiki therapy without the risk of side effects or complications.

Preventing Future Ailments

Reiki not only provides healing for current and past issues that affect your physical, mental, emotional, and spiritual state. It also strengthens your body against future ailments. It offers aid for potential health conditions.

Aligning the Chakras

Chakras are referred to as energy centers found within and all-around entities. They cannot be seen physically; however, they affect the systems of the body. A blocked chakra impedes the energy flow in an individual. Thus, it may cause physical, mental, and emotional disturbance. Reiki opens up the chakras, tears down blockages, and returns the chakras into a balanced state. Some people's chakras may be extremely imbalanced due to past traumas, illnesses, accidents and other negative life experiences. Reiki is a great opportunity to get up, brush oneself off and have a new, fresh start. <u>Everyone in the world should be allowed a second chance, right?</u>

Other benefits of Reiki therapy include the following:

- Promotes relaxation and stress reduction

- Aids in better sleep

- Improves the natural healing abilities of the body

- Improves overall health

- Brings inner peace, harmony, and spiritual growth

- Balances the mind and emotions

- Provides a more peaceful state of being

- Provides mental balance for learning, mental clarity, and memory

- Strengthens and heals personal relationships

- Enhances ability to love

- Improves capacity for empathy

- Offers relief for sorrow or emotional distress

- Relieves physical pain caused by migraine, sciatica, arthritis, etc.

- Speeds up recovery from long-term illness or surgery

- Reduces side effects of medicines or medical procedures, among others

I am sure that right now you just can't wait to start!

So, let's do it!

Let's start with some amazing pre-Reiki exercises that will help you become aware of your energy. I suggest you do them every day from today on. For optimal results, do them twice a day, whenever you have some spare moments and won't be disturbed. You can also do them with your friend, partner, spouse, family member or even colleague. They will thank you later...You already know about the White-Purple Light pre-Reiki exercise, and I encourage you to let it help you as much as you need.

Below are more fantastic tools for you:

1. ***Strong Tree***

Stand barefoot on the floor. Leave some space between your feet. If you can do this exercise on a fresh grass or sand, somewhere in nature, like woods, mountains or beach, that's even better! But don't worry if for now you are stuck in your apartment and can't treat yourself to such a luxury. Simply do it and practise it now and as soon as you can, you can do it somewhere nice, outdoors.

Close your eyes.

Rotate your head and your hips in order to feel relaxed. Allow all the tension leave your body. Shake your hands breathing energetically to let negativity leave your body. Stretch for a few minutes if you need to. Remember to breathe in deeply, in through your nose and out through your mouth.

Now, raise your hands up, as if you were trying to touch the sky. Keep breathing. As you do this, your hands should be in this position (as if you were to fill them with some liquid):

Now, slowly lower your hands, palms facing upwards. You are collecting the Universal energy through your hands. Keep breathing and feel your belly moving with each breath.

Now, focus on your feet. The sensation you get in the palms of your feet as they touch the ground. Focus your attention on how they connect you to the Earth. Now, imagine yourself as a tree. Feel your feet and picture them as roots of an amazingly strong tree. No matter what happens, you remain unperturbed. You may start feeling a nice, warming sensation in your feet. If not, don't worry, everyone is different and so are their sensations...

Keep visualizing yourself as a tree. Now, picture a white, big ball of light, just underneath the ground, it's tangled with the roots that connect to your feet. The light travels up to your feet and then crosses all your body, in all directions.

Relax your hands and raise them above your head again.

Now place them on your eyes. Again, you may start feeling warmth, but if not, don't worry.

Finally, imagine the same white light entering your head. Now you feel protected and enlightened from the inside out.

If you want, take it one step further...

Sit down on a chair, or in a lotus position. Relax, and start placing your hands on your head, neck, abdomen gently hovering your hands about 1-2 inches from your body and finally landing on your beautiful body to bring peace and healing. Touch the areas that are in pain and need more attention. If you have sore eyes after working on a computer, place your hands on them and breathe in and out. Place your hands on your neck if you feel like.

How does it feel? Are you now more aware of your subtle energy? Feel free to let me know in the review section of this book...

2. **Chakra breathing**- even though we won't be focusing on any specific chakras yet, we will practise a rather unusual

way of breathing- in and out through your mouth at all times.

For me, it symbolizes breaking away from old concepts and conventions as well as cultivating new habits and beliefs. In everyday life, we are very often too scared of the unknown and stick to what we already know. Maybe sometimes it can make us happy to try something new? Whether it's a new route to drive to your food store, or work, or visit a new place for a weekend (even though it's near where you live), or try a new workout, or go out and talk to strangers? Whatever it is, it means leaving your comfort zone.

Again, this is just my personal opinion, take it if you like it, and reject it if it's not for you...

Sit down comfortably, preferably in lotus or semi-lotus position.

First take a few deep breaths in and out, the way that feels right for you. Now, start breathing in and out through your mouth.

If you have any existing health conditions, please consult your physician first before applying this breathing method. If, during this practise, you feel dizzy or short of breath, please stop and return to normal breathing.

At first, it will feel unusual to breathe in and out your mouth. Keep doing it and observe your body. Do you feel like there are any obstacles, anything that prevents you from breathing in and out through your mouth? Don't be afraid to make deep breathing noises. It will help you purify your energy field. As you breathe, observe your belly. While you breathe in, it goes up and relaxes. While you breathe out, you feel it shrink.

3. Warm hands energy

Sit on a chair or in a lotus position.

Raise your hand above your head, palms facing upwards.

Take a few deep breaths and make an intention to connect to the universal healing energy.

Now, take the right hand down, very slowly, and place it around your solar plexus zone. Allow the left hand to join the right hand and keep this position for a few minutes.

Now, place the hands in a prayer position. Keep breathing. Now, slowly move your hands from each other, leaving a space of a few inches.

Keep moving them away slowly, and then back together (without them touching each other) again. Repeat a few times.

Do you feel warmth? Do you feel your energy?

Now, find the spot that needs attention, it may be neck muscles in pain, sore throat, or tired eyesight. Simply place your hands on those spots (use slow, gentle movements). Let them hover an inch or two above your body and then land on the area treated and keep your hands on them. Observe your body. Simply give it intention, and it will come.

This is what you have just learned (and practiced) about Reiki:

- The astonishing body, mind and spirit benefits of Reiki are unlimited;
- The fact that you use Reiki on yourself or ask a Reiki healer to help your health does not mean you should dispose of

standard medical treatments or advice. Everything is necessary and there is a reason for everything. Standard medicine and its research cannot be rejected, as you can always combine it with Reiki;

- Three simple pre-Reiki exercises to help you dive into the ocean of spiritual wellness and healing...

Don't worry if you could not concentrate or did not feel anything. Just keep going, take baby steps. Even if you don't feel anything as you do those pre-Reiki steps at this stage, you will certainly feel the benefits later down the road. Think about it as investing in yourself and creating the biggest spiritual asset you possibly could.

Now, I hope you are ready for the next chapter. If you feel like you still need to go back, and allow yourself to re-do the previous exercises, go for it. Listen to your heart and intuition. Don't force yourself to finish this book sooner that you are meant to. Don't let your ego decide what's good for you. Let your spirit decide what it needs.

Maybe what you really want right now is to go outside and spend some time in nature, where you can connect to the universal energy and feel the healing power that you were born with, yet was possibly left dormant for so many years.

Whatever you decide to do, I will be waiting for you to help you move on with the rest of this journey...

Chapter 4: Reiki and the Subtle Energy - How Reiki Actually Works and How You Can Make It Work for You and Your Loved Ones

The general concept of Reiki is healing through a transfer of the life force energy from a Reiki practitioner to another individual. The life force energy is channelled through a practitioner's hands while holding another individual at specific points to facilitate recovery response. In some instances, Reiki is practiced at a distance where the patient or receiver is not physically present with the practitioner.

A practitioner who has successfully completed the Reiki 2 level and has been able to practise it plus has a distance healing intention, will be able to help you in exactly the same way, as if he or she were to do a normal treatment. You now know and understand that Reiki is a non-invasive healing practice that can be used to prevent or cure imbalances in the body. We have also mentioned that a Reiki healer uses the universal energy, working as a channel and remaining humble at all times.

The Reiki Theory – How It Works

According to many studies on Reiki, it works through a subtle energy, which is infinite, and within all entities. This subtle energy is organized into energy fields and systems within and between individuals and the environment, allowing the life force energy to be channelled or transferred.

The Reiki practitioner channels or transfers the subtle energy (the universal energy) to help activate as well as enhance an individual's natural healing abilities. The power or energy channelled may also be transferred to other entities apart from humans. Plants and animals can also receive this energy. I also told you that it can be sent to the past or the future (remember my stories?). Some people even send it to the deceased, especially if there was no opportunity to say goodbye to them before they left this world).

The life force energy provides balance between the mind and the body. It serves as a holistic healing method. On the other hand, some researchers argue that no such energy exists, and that Reiki only focuses on the effects of this energy rather than its existence. No matter what you decide to believe, you can receive Reiki as long as you allow it to heal you.

You don't need to believe in it, you just need to allow it. For example, let's say I want to offer you a Reiki session. You say yes, but you tell me you don't believe it. That's fine, and you can still experience its benefits, no matter what your beliefs are. However, if you tell me you don't want to receive it, I should not try to Reiki-treat you without your consent. Reiki's principles respect individual's needs and choices. <u>You should never try to work Reiki on a person who does not want it.</u>

In the Reiki System, illness refers to a blockage in the energy field of an individual, which is put back into balance through the healing force, resulting in health improvement of the physical body. Reiki practitioners learn and undergo training to be open to the availability of the life force energy. It's a life-long study. As such, the practitioner does not need a conscious effort to activate the healing powers of Reiki, which is channelled to another individual. Based on this premise, Reiki healing does not come from the Reiki practitioner or master. Reiki itself facilitates the process of self-healing of the individual.

Moreover, like I told you in the introduction, Reiki does not require physiological or anatomical background in order to practice the healing method on oneself or on others. It does not require a previous knowledge of massage or manipulation technique.

The Reiki Healing Session – How It Is Done

The original Reiki System founded by Misao Usui involves 12 hand positions to start a session, hand positions for covering the main chakras of the head and trunk, and the use of a head-to-toe approach. Thus, a designated set of hand positions is used as a method to carry out Reiki.

These hand positions touch different body parts while the patient or the receiver of Reiki is standing, sitting, or lying down and fully clothed. Reiki can also be carried out as a distant healing in which a patient or the receiver of Reiki is not necessarily physically present during a session.

During such a session, a Reiki healer simply visualizes you and performs exactly the same steps they would do if they were with you physically. Personally, I have never done the distance healing as a practitioner; however I have experienced it as a patient. I talk about my first Reiki experiences in my book: "Exploring Chakras and Discovering Holistic Wellness".

For at least five minutes, the practitioner's hands remain in each appointed position. Usually, with more experience, the practitioner follows his/her intuition on where to put his/her hands for the energy to flow at a particular position. They can feel where the imbalances occur in your body. In a session for treating others, the practitioner sits just above the head of a massage table or bed and starts with the appointed hand positions for the head. He/she gently moves his/her hands down the body and returns to the area of pain, distress, or tension after a while.

Of course, different practitioners have different techniques. If you decide to do the Reiki 1 Level, you will probably be given a manual-something like a set of hand positions to stick to. In most cases, you will be asked to stick to your guide, usually until you move to the Reiki 2 level. At least, this is how I was taught by my master and this is how he was taught. The reason is simple- it's about acquiring and automating a certain set of skills so that we can just perform them without thinking too much about it. With more practise, you usually let your intuition guide you.

Advanced practitioners may alter the order of hand positions depending on the needs of the patient and the spontaneity of the energy flow in the body of the patient. A typical Reiki session lasts between an hour and hour and a half, but this is subject to change. While receiving Reiki, your perception of time may change, or you may fall asleep.

You can use exactly the same hand positions to heal yourself and you can also use them to help others.

In a traditional manner, a practitioner completes three levels or degrees in the Reiki System training to become a Reiki Master.

The only requirement prior to the commencement of the training is the practitioner's desire to learn as well as a commitment to utilize Reiki based on its original intention. Although Reiki can be learned and accessed by everyone, an individual may be prevented from connecting with it due to a history of physical, mental, or emotional difficulty.

As such, each level in the Reiki System training involves a set of attunement or initiation to open blocked energy fields and enhance the channels of energy within the practitioner.

In its traditional form, teaching Reiki is done through oral lectures, meaning the practitioner is only guided by his intuition and the Reiki Master.

There were no textbooks or tangible materials that serve as a guide for practitioners. This is probably the reason why through the years, Reiki had a number of variations based on the original practice.

How Reiki Changes One's Life

Reiki can change one's life in an extremely profound way. Its overwhelming effects begin when an individual decides to learn and commit himself/herself to utilize Reiki.

Reiki opens many new horizons for an individual's physical, mental, emotional, and spiritual levels. This art of healing provides an individual the ability to view events, things, or people positively regardless of the situation. For instance, a person who experiences Reiki can take a petty grievance as it is and not as something that would cloud his/her emotions.

Reiki can also unclog an individual's mind from stress and tension and make them, instead, view life while looking at the bigger picture. Thus, Reiki can change one's life through setting him/her free from physical, mental, emotional, and spiritual negativity.

Reiki is truly a powerful art of healing, as it reawakens your perspective of YOUR true purpose. It provides you with better clarity of thoughts, emotions, and actions, which affirms your natural ability to heal and be healed.

Reiki can change lives as one becomes aware of his/her spiritual self through the life force energy. It can also free you from any inhibition and develop clarity in mind and emotions. When you live in balance through Reiki, it can inspire you to make changes in various aspects of your life. These changes all lead to the direction of finding your true self and alleviated life.

Before we jump into chakras and balancing them, I want to show you a few practical Reiki exercises and techniques you can start doing straight away. These are usually taught during the Reiki Level 1 course, and I believe it's better to master them before we dive in the world of chakras. This is a simple, step-by-step, walk-through to help you experience Reiki whenever and wherever you want.

Activate the Reiki Energy with Hatsurei-Ho

Hatsurei-Ho is one of the basic methods of Reiki and it means, "emanate universal energy." It serves as a tool to purify your energy and be ready for the highest good. It actually consists of several different techniques, that when performed on a regular basis, can help you achieve and maintain holistic wellness.

Here's what Hatsurei-Ho energy-cleansing healing ritual consists of:

1. *Kihon Shisei*

Sit down comfortably in a Japanese style position (Sei Za)

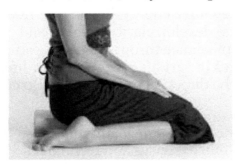

Alternatively, you can sit down in a lotus position or on a chair with your legs touching the ground. I usually prefer lotus position.

IMPORTANT: don't sit down with your legs crossed. The only acceptable variation is the lotus pose (the energy circulates freely). Make sure your back is straight, but don't force it. You must feel comfortable.

Make sure all the electronic devices around you are switched off (no silence mode- simply switch them off. It's good to go off technology sometimes, which is a topic for another book).

Close your eyes and focus on your breath and the lower chakras and a spot 1-2 inches below your navel.

Place both of your hands on your thighs, palms facing upwards.

2. *Mokunen- Talk to your subconscious mind*

This step is simply about concentrating and putting all your focus on Hatsurei-Ho. Simply tell your subconscious, "I am ready to activate Reiki with Hatsurei-Ho." Place your intention and be grateful for this amazing opportunity.

3. *Ken'Yoku- Dry bathing that helps you get rid of all kinds of toxins, including mental and emotional. You can use it anytime you are exposed to negative energies.*

Place the fingers of your right hand on your left shoulder.

Now, slide your hand down, diagonally to your right hip. Make the movement fast and while you make it, say "haaa," and don't be afraid to make some noise.

You want to get rid of all negative energy. This sound is very liberating. It's actually called: *Hado respiration*.

Now, place the fingers of your left hand on your right shoulder and slide it down diagonally all the way to your left hip saying "haa."

Repeat the first step again: Place the fingers of your right hand on your left shoulder and slide your hand down, diagonally to your right hip. Again, accompany this rapid movement by "haa" sound.

Place your hands on your thighs again, palms facing upwards.

4. *Connect to Reiki*

Since we have already done some pre-Reiki exercises, it will be much easier for you to connect.

Gently raise your hands above your head. Tell your subconscious: *I am connecting to Reiki healing energy now.*

Feel Reiki in all cells of your body.

5. *Joshin Kokyu Ho- Energize your mind and soul with breathing techniques*

Breathe in through your nose, out through your mouth.

Place your hands on your thighs, palms facing upwards, as if you were to collect water or other liquids in it.

Keep breathing and focus all your attention on the air moving your belly up and down. Keep breathing and maintain this position for at least five minutes.

Now imagine the white Reiki light entering the crown of your head and moving down to your heart and expanding warm, healing energy to all parts of your body.

Direct the special healing to the areas that really need it. As you breathe out the air, you may say "haa" (Hado respiration from the previous steps). Carry on as long as you feel is right for you and your soul.

6. *Gassho technique to calm down your mind*

Gassho means: "palms of your hands together" and it expresses gratitude.

Put your hands together, like in the picture below. Your hands should be in front of your heart. Keep breathing in through your nose and out through your mouth. Focus all your attention on middle fingers of each hand. Your hands may start sweating and you may start experiencing a nice, warming and pulsating sensation in your body. This is normal. Embrace it.

7. *Seishin Toitsu- Concentrate your mind*

Keep your hands in gassho position. Keep breathing. Now, as you breathe in, imagine the white healing Reiki light enter your hands and flowing to your navel area (1-2 inches below). Keep breathing and visualizing and stay in this position as long as feels right for you. Finally, say (preferably out loud) the Reiki Principles: *Just for today I am free from anger, I am free from worry, I am humble, I am honest, I am compassionate about myself and others.* Repeat a few times.

8. *Mokunen- conclusion (silent communication with your subconscious mind)*

Place your hands on your thighs, palms facing upwards and say to your subconscious (3 times): *I have finished Hatsurei-Ho now, and I am grateful to the Universe for providing me with this amazing healing energy.*

Make sure you go through all of the steps as much as you need to. You will be using the above-mentioned techniques to connect to the Universal Energy, so that you can get more benefits from other tools I am just about to share with you. Keep reading and healing! The best is yet to come!

Chapter 5: Explore Your Chakras, Realize Your Weak Points and Balance Yourself with Reiki. Simple Healing Techniques You Wish You Had Known Years Ago!

Chakras reside in the subtle or spiritual body and are part of one's energy system. There are seven main chakras used in the Reiki System. They run from a base of your spine to the top of your head.

There are also many minor chakras, which is a topic for another book. For now, all you need to do is to understand, feel and take care of the main seven chakras in your beautiful body. Once you have gotten the hang of it and how it feels, you will be able to transfer your wisdom so as to help others create balanced lifestyles.

However, for now, you need to focus on yourself. You need to start a self-healing journey first, so that when you are more balanced, you can go and do a great job in the world.

The seven main chakras correlate to your endocrine glandular system, which is responsible for the regulation of hormones in your body.

The hormones, on the other hand, have a contributory factor of your general health and well-being. In fact, the hormone regulation controls some of the most critical processes in the body.

Some of these processes include your growth, aging, stress reactions, metabolism, reproductive systems, and healing among others.

The role of the chakras is aligning the seven major endocrine glands. In a Reiki session, the endocrine glands, which are the physical body and the chakras, are also the energetic body filled with the life force energy or *Chi* to bring about balance.

Chakras affect your daily life. This is to say that a positive experience can affect the state of the chakras positively, while a negative experience can disrupt the state of the chakras and cause imbalance. For instance, when you receive a hug from a loved one, it can affect your chakras; in this case, the heart and sacral chakras. These chakras will receive beneficial energy and spread it evenly resulting in your feeling of love and happiness.

On the other hand, when your go through a negative experience, the chakras can be disrupted, resulting in the feeling of unpleasantness or discomfort.

When the chakra is balanced, it moves in a circular motion and constitutes feelings of contentment and wholeness. A chakra that is highly functioning also results in the body's vitality and good health. However, when a chakra is weak and unbalanced, the body demonstrates a lack of energy, depression, and restlessness. It also results in a feeling of disconnection.

This chapter provides the basic information on chakras. All you need to know to get started on Reiki. If you wish to continue your chakra journey, you may be interested in reading my book: "Exploring Chakras and Discovering Holistic Wellness." For now, don't worry, this program contains all you need to know to carry on your spiritual research. However, if you want to take it to the next level and have a look at your chakras and realize possible imbalances, you may be interested in reading my other book from the series. In case you are already familiar with chakras, the following paragraphs will serve you as consolidation. Reinforcement of what you already know can make you apply the information faster and more efficiently, hence more holistic wellness for you.

The Seven Main Chakras

The Root Chakra - The first chakra is the Root chakra or the Muladhara. It is located between the spine's base and the pubic bone. The Root chakra is associated with the family relationships or tribal connections of people.

This means that it is related to where people come from. It is associated with the sense of smell; the element earth; the musical note of C; and the color red. The Root chakra regulates your physical identity, instincts, family or social honor, survival, and security. When it is balanced, the Root chakra can provide you with a sense of being grounded to the Earth. On the other hand, an imbalance in the Root chakra manifests in low energy, fatigue, greed, obesity, and recklessness.

The Sacral Chakra - The second chakra is the Sacral chakra or the Svadisthana. It is located a few inches below the navel. The Sacral chakra is associated with your relationships with others. It regulates your creativity, self-gratification, physical sensations, sexual energy, desires, addictions, and movement.

The Sacral chakra keeps people connected through their feelings. It provides you with the ability to give and receive on various levels of sensuality, intimacy, and creativity with others. This chakra is associated with the element water, which represents emotions, the sense of taste, the musical note of D, and the color orange. When the Sacral chakra is

71

balanced, it enhances your relationships and connections with other people. An imbalance in this chakra, however, manifests impotence, frigidity, promiscuity, and blocks creativity.

The Solar Plexus Chakra - The third chakra is the Solar Plexus or the Manipura. It is located just above your navel. The Solar Plexus chakra is associated with one's relationship to himself/herself. It is associated with the sense of sight, the element fire, the musical note of E, and the color yellow. The Solar Plexus chakra regulates your sense of self-esteem, personality, intuition, and ego. When it is balanced, the Solar Plexus chakra allows you to easily achieve goals as well as discern personal desires and will.

On the other hand, an imbalance in the Solar Plexus chakra manifests aggression, high levels of stress, control issues, and complacency. Other key issues involved with this chakra include self-definition, anxiety, will, self honor, personal power, fear, opinion formation, and introversion.

The Heart Chakra - The fourth chakra is the Heart chakra or the Anahata. It is located in the chest's center. The Heart chakra is associated with compassion, harmony, unconditional love, well-being, equilibrium, and the union of energies of male and female. It is associated with the sense of touch, the air element, the musical note of F, and the color green.

When it is balanced, the Heart chakra can provide the feeling of peace, be in harmony with oneself and others, nurture strengths, and follow the heart's impulse. On the other hand, an imbalance in the Heart chakra manifests co-dependency, distrust, selfishness, smothering, and emotional imbalance.

The Throat Chakra - The fifth chakra is the Throat chakra or the Vishuddha. It is located in the body's neck and mouth areas. The Throat chakra is associated with one's growth and communication through expression. It is associated with the senses of hearing and speaking, the element ether, the musical note of G, and the color blue.

The Throat chakra regulates your language, independence, self-expression, and sound vibration. When it is balanced, the Throat chakra allows you to connect thoughts and emotions easily and choose compassion over judgment of self and others.

On the other hand, an imbalance in the Throat chakra manifests in inability to speak and listen, inability to make clear and conscious choices, too much talking, and being disputative.

The Brow Chakra - The sixth chakra is the Brow chakra or the Anja. It is located between the eyebrows. The Brow chakra is associated with balancing the lower and higher self and your ability to trust your inner guidance. It is associated with the senses of sight and extra sensory perception (ESP), the element air, the musical note of A, and the colors purple or indigo.

The Brow chakra is the seat of one's intuition. It is where your higher self resides. When it is balanced, the Brow chakra manifests truth, seeing or perceiving things through the big picture, and self-reflection. On the other hand, an imbalance in the Brow chakra manifests in forgetfulness, being illogical, racing thoughts, migraines or headaches, and inability to recall dreams.

The Crown Chakra - The seventh chakra is the Crown chakra or the Saharara. It is located on the top of the head. The Crown chakra is associated with your pure consciousness, divine self-knowledge, highest thought, universal identity, and your connection to the greater world beyond.

It is related to the element light, the musical note of B, and the colors violet or white. The Crown chakra connects the rest of the chakras through honoring a higher power. When it is balanced, it allows you to live in the present and seek wisdom, clarity, and truth.

On the other hand, an imbalance in the Crown chakra manifests in lack of a higher purpose, lack of spiritual awareness, and the feeling of being spaced out.

Basic Steps in Balancing the Seven Main Chakras with Reiki

Reiki is an efficient method of balancing as well as enhancing the seven main chakras or the energy centers. There are many of ways and protocols to practise Reiki.

Now, I want to show you the most basic and simplest one. I urge you to stop reading and practise these steps. All you need is intention. Give yourself some well-deserved balance and holistic relaxation. Take your time and feel the universal energy in all your cells. It's free. It always has been and always will be. And it will help you make your worries go away. So what are you waiting for? <u>Who doesn't want to be happy?</u>

Everyone can practice the following exercise. It doesn't matter if you are a Reiki practitioner or master, or have never even heard of it. It's all about utilizing and taking advantage of an amazing self-healing tool that is always there for you, no matter where you are, what your social status is, how much money you have in your bank account, or if you were a good or a bad person in the past.

Remember, everyone deserves a second chance. <u>Reiki and self-love go hand in hand</u>. Their other friends are self-acceptance and forgiveness. Very often, before you can forgive others, or let them forgive you, you need to forgive yourself first. Let the judgment go. You are creating a new, balanced you.

This is a new chapter of your book of life, and the writer is you! You are in charge of your life now. Having Reiki on board is a great gift. Knowing that it has always been there for you, but you did not know about it, can even make you feel a bit impatient...I get the feeling. This is why we should get started on chakra balancing exercises straight away!

Before you start, I suggest you connect to Reiki by following the Hatsurei-Ho Ritual. You will be amazingly prepared to balance your chakras with the Universal Energy.

Preparation:

Step 1

The first step in balancing the chakras involves lying down on the back with one hand placed on the forehead (6th chakra). The other hand is placed over the pubic bone (1st chakra). Your hands should rest in these positions for at least five minutes. This step balances your energy from your head to the lower body parts and allows you to be more connected with your sexual energy. Raise your hand slightly (1-2 inches) off your body and gently lower them down again so that they touch your 6th and 1st chakra. Repeat a few times. One thing is sure: you will feel amazingly relaxed. You can thank me later!

Step 2

The second step in balancing the chakras: keep lying down with one hand moving over the throat (5th chakra) while the other to the belly just below the navel (2nd chakra). Your hands should rest in these positions for at least five minutes. This step allows you to balance your emotions and vitality specifically in terms of communication and self-expression. This will also help you become more in touch with your emotions and desires. It will likewise enhance your creativity in terms of expression. Again, let the hands hover over the chakras and slowly place them on them. Choose whatever feels right for you. Don't get too obsessed about "steps to follow." Listen to your heart if necessary.

Step 3

The third step in balancing the chakras: keep moving one hand to the center of the chest (4th chakra) while the other to the solar plexus (3rd chakra). This step allows you to use love and understanding in making decisions. This is because the Heart Chakra is associated with love and compassion while the Solar Plexus chakra is associated with personal power and strength. The combination of both is what makes a great leader who wants the best for his or her community.

Step 4

The fourth step in balancing the chakras: keep moving one hand to the belly across the navel at the Sacral chakra (2nd chakra). The other hand should be placed on the forehead in the third eye area (6th chakra). Just like the first step but with "switched hands". Your beautiful hands should rest in these positions for at least five minutes. This step allows you to let go of his/her thoughts and feelings. It will also provide you with the feeling of deep relaxation.

The fifth and final step in balancing the chakras involves stretching your entire body, wiggling the toes and fingers, and coming back to your natural consciousness. This step marks the end of balancing the chakras.

Here's another exercise. You have already practised the chakra breathing with the basic, simplified technique in the previous chapters. In case you don't remember, it involved breathing in and out through your mouth. Don't be afraid to make funny noses if you feel like it. Sometimes, you may feel like shouting so as to get rid of negative emotions that were negatively affecting your chakras' wellbeing.

Now, let's take it to the next level. After connecting to Reiki, stand up and relax your body by stretching for a few minutes and breathing the way that feels right for you. Now, allow a bit of space between your legs. Close your eyes and start breathing in and out through your mouth.

You will be hovering your hands above the 7 major chakras- first from the first one to the seventh, and then all the way down.

The recommended hands positions are:

Place the right hand first near the first chakra (without touching the body, your hands should be about 1-2 inches from your chakras) and cover it with the left hand. Make sure that the hands don't touch each other. Again, leave 1-2 inches of space between two hands.

Start with the first chakra. Hover above it using both hands. Breathe in and out. When you are ready, move the right hand up on to the second chakra and once it's on it (not literally, but 1-2 inches from your body) move the left hand above your right hand. Continue to breath in and out through your mouth. Keep moving up. First the right hand, then the left hand joining the right hand and the right hand moving up again.

You will finally move to the crown chakra. From there, you start moving down again, until you reach the first chakra. The process is the same. First the right hand, then the left.

I am sure there are some variations. I am just telling you the way I was taught. It's quite probable you will create your own way in the process—that's totally fine. You don't need to copy exactly what I do. As long as you have the intention, and you listen to your heart, you are good to go.

Experiences that people have during this exercise:

Some people realize chakra blockages in their body. Some people even feel like laughing or crying. Past events and traumas may arise, but only to be healed eventually. Make sure to drink lots of pure, filtered, preferably alkaline ionized water before and after you do this technique.

What are Auras?

Now that you have an understanding of what a chakra is, it
will be easier for you to grasp the concept of what an aura
is and how they interrelate. The chakras are essentially
energy gates of the aura. They keep our auras luminous
and vivid, and when they are in balance, they will keep us
healthy and happy. Chakras are a powerful tool to attain
true holistic wellness, and I hope that you investigate them
further.

Auras:

Aura, sounds like a mystical, supernatural, hocus pocus,
bunch of non-sense to some. In all actuality, the aura is
very real. It is simply the natural energy of your body, put
out by the chakras, radiating around you. Auras are out
own personal energy field. The world and people around us
are affected by our energy of the aura. If you pay close
attention, you can feel the energy of another person when
they are close to you, in your personal space (aura).

Auras can actually be seen as a "glowing egg" of color,
glowing around the human body. The color of one's aura is
determined by the strongest chakras, although, the color is
a mixture of all your chakra light energy. Everyone's aura
can be seen as any one of the colors in the rainbow. They
appear as different hues and shades, each one having a
different meaning regarding emotion, spirituality, and
health.

Auras are comprised of an equal amount of layers,
regardless of color. Layers differ in deepness and
transparency. Most often, seven layers are seen, although it
is possible for certain people to decipher nine. There is a
possibility that more layers exist, but have not currently

been defined.

Each chakra corresponds to a layer of the aura and are listed from 1-7, from close to the body, moving outward. Oddly enough (no pun intended), layers 1,3,5, and 7 have a tendency to be more well configured, while 2,4, and 6 are more iridescent, fluctuating, and fluid. The higher the number, the higher the vibration is, this causes a current of energy that moves vertically, pulsing up and out to the perimeter of the aura. The healthier the individual, and the more open the chakras, the further that the aura can extend off of the body.

1. Etheric: Ether is the space that is between energy and matter, from the planets to the stars, even the space between atoms. This layer ranges from a ¼ in. to 2 in. away from the edge of our physical body. The etheric layer is the medium to which our own skin is affixed. It is made up of little, delicate, threads of energy that are interwoven around the body. It is almost a copy of your skin, yet it is made of energy. Flickers of energy travel through this matrix, sparkling as they flow. Many well-practiced aura viewers can see this web of energy. Beginners may only view a muted, blurry, transparent vapor, kind of like you see coming off of the ground on an extremely hot day. May people have seen it, even if they have never tried to view an aura. It can be seen as a grey to blue fog to a novice, to sparks of blue or grey light by the well-trained eye. Active people tend to have more of a grey color, while those who are more inactive have more of a blue coloring.

    The Etheric Layer is interconnected with the Root Chakra and what we experience through our five senses. This means that both physical pain and pleasure have an effect on the Etheric Body. What we eat and the way that we exercise (or lack of exercise) has an influence on it as well.

The way that we feel (or vibe) other's energy also takes place in the Etheric Body. The energy here throbs at a rate near 20 cycles every 60 seconds.

2. Emotional: Aptly named, this layer deals with our feelings and emotions. The Emotional Layer reaches out 1-3 in. from the physical body. It is a fluid layer that permeates all of the other layers. The unformulated flames of color do not resemble the shape of our physical body. The colors of the Emotional Body fluctuate in response to the emotion being felt at the time. The colors range from vivid thanks to positive emotion, to muddy in response to negative emotion. It is possible to see every color in this layer, and it is usually the first layer of color that someone first learns to see.

    Intertwined with the Sacral Chakra, the Emotional Body is connected to how we perceive ourselves, and how those perceptions make us feel. In order to keep this layer thriving, it is important to vent and feel those emotions regardless of what they are. Do not hold them in or ignore them.

3. Mental: Like the Etheric Layer, this layer is more defined and configured. It is found 3-8 in. away from the physical body. The Mental Body is usually seen as yellow or gold in color, and is brightest between the head and the shoulders. The radiance of the light in this layer is brightest while concentrating and focusing on a mental task. Sometimes sparks and splotches of colors are seen are seen when one creates repetitive thought patterns. These color differences are dictated by how a person is connected emotionally to their thought processes.

    Our Mental Layer interacts with the Solar Plexus Chakra. It

is interrelated with both left and right brain capabilities. The equal use of both sides of the brain, logical and imaginative, will keep the Mental Body in good health. Daydreaming, lucid dreaming, the active use of the imagination, active learning, and the quest for knowledge are all things that we can do to achieve this well-being. The Mental Layer is susceptible to serious destruction if one stays in a state of negativity or cynical thinking for too long.

4. Astral: This vaporous layer is full of color, reaching out 1-1 ½ ft. outside the body. The Astral Layer is where we create astral cords that connect us to others, whether they are positive or negative, current or previous connections. The Astral Body is the area of the aura where we pick up on the vibes (vibrations) of others. It is usually bathed in a pinkish color due to the formation of romantic or plutonic relationships are created. Many chakras can be seen in the Astral Layer, but usually have a pink hue.

   The Astral Layer is a long term collection of how we feel about ourselves, on both an emotional and intellectual level. It is the connection linking experiences. The Astral Body rules visualization, dreaming, and hallucinating. You are mentally aware of this part of yourself, but at the same time, you can still come into contact with other levels of reality. The Astral Body allows us to project, and be in two places at the same time.

   The Astral Layer is connected to the Heart Chakra. This connection links us to relations with others, and how these associations have an influence on our emotions. The way to keep this layer functioning at its best is by keeping healthy, encouraging, constructive relationships with people and the world around us.

5. Etheric Template: This layer is located around 1 ½-2 ft. outside of the body. The Etheric Template is actually a structured blueprint/master plan of everything that is alive on the physical level. It is a negative of the Etheric Layer, a dark blue background with thin, light energy streaks. When something is wrong with the Etheric Layer, you can go into your Etheric Template to find out how to rebalance.

This template is connected to the Throat Chakra, the place where noise is turned into matter. The Etheric Template is where divine will and the power of manifesting your will into existence are formed. Devine will is established by our inner, higher self and is the greatest longing for a direction in our existence that will serve a greater good. By aligning our free and divine wills, we can have a healthy, vivid Etheric Template Layer. When these two wills are not lined up, this layer will still have energy lines, but they will not be as plentiful nor as bright. This will cause you to feel as if you are wandering in life without purpose. By using the power of manifestation in relation to your divine and free will, you can rebalance this layer by changing your reality and existence.

6. Celestial: While the Etheric Layer is more of a physical form of the higher self, the Celestial Layer is the emotional form of the higher self. It is located about 2-2 ¾ ft. outside of the body. The colors in the Celestial Body are iridescent and pastel, almost like a bubble or an abalone shell. In this layer we have a connection to a higher power and generate unconditional love that attaches us to other physical beings. It generates energy, much like a star or the sun, radiating outward.

The Celestial Body is associated with the Third Eye Chakra. It reflects our connections, on a spiritual level, with the universe. We can keep this layer healthy by practicing meditation, present moment awareness, and by pondering religion, spirituality, or the philosophies of reality and existence. The Celestial Layer is where we view the divine and spiritual nature within ourselves and in those around us. It also connected to each individual's awareness of the divine and how sensitive and open we are to the spiritual realm.

7. Ketheric Template: Extending 2 ½-3 ft. away from the body, this layer is where we become aware of the fact that we are one with our higher power and the universe. Its outer edge is the toughest, most durable layer. The Ketheric Layer is oval in shape, like an egg. Comprised of thin, pulsating golden threads, it also supplies the energy that runs through the spine, powering the entire body. The higher-self fills the Ketheric Body and this can be seen by way of a gold glow. It is the intellectual layer of the spiritual realm. Here in the Ketheric Layer we are joined with the universal mind and are able to comprehend it, as well as being able understand past lives.

    The Ketheric Body is intertwined with the Crown Chakra, and connects us to the universal mind. We can keep this layer healthy by understanding, and having insights regarding our place in the universal mind and our connection to the divine. This is achieved by having contact with higher power and having spiritual experiences. We can strengthen the Ketheric Body by constantly seeking out divine wisdom, knowledge, and ideas.

Chapter 6: Reiki and Its Amazing, Powerful Exercises for Wellness, Health, and Abundance–the Practical ABC's!

As you already know, apart from physical healing, Reiki can be also used to help you recharge and rejuvenate you to a mental, emotional, and spiritual level as well. In this chapter we will have a look at other Reiki healing techniques for unlimited holistic wellness. Before commencing on any of the following techniques, I suggest connect to Reiki using the Hatsurei-Ho technique from Chapter 4.

Reiki Exercise for Wellness

This exercise starts by you making yourself comfortable. You can either sit or lie on your back with eyes closed. The key is to pay attention to your breathing while following its rhythm. Observe how your breathing flows in and out. Next, place your hands on the area of your body where you feel tension or you feel drawn to. In this step, you should be able to make use of your intuition in locating the area of your body that needs relaxation.

The next step is to direct your breath repeatedly and consciously to the affected area of your body. The key is to imagine your breath as the life force energy that flows incessantly through you. Imagine collecting your breath/energy and expanding it into your hands. You will feel the energy spreading out from your hands throughout the other parts of your body. Remain in this position for at least five minutes.

Then, put your hands on another area of your body. Breathe into your hands and repeat steps one to three. You may notice that your breathing changes as you switch positions. This means that the stored experiences and memories in your body are now awakened.

You may feel the energy better if you allow yourself to go with the flow. After going through other areas of your body, open your eyes slowly. Stretch and return to natural consciousness. This exercise will provide you the feeling of calmness. It can also make you more focused and relaxed.

Reiki Exercises for Health

Quick Energizer Method - This Reiki exercise is intended to replenish depleted energy. It aims to provide you with the feeling of being refreshed and renewed energy.

The first step is to sit or lie down in a comfortable place. Place one of your hands over the third chakra or the Solar Plexus while the other, directly touching your stomach.

Next, relax your hands while closing your eyes. Let your mind rest. Remain in this position for about 10-15 minutes.

After this exercise, you will feel refreshed and rejuvenated with ample energy.

Sleeping Aid

This Reiki exercise for health is intended for individuals who have trouble sleeping at night. It will encourage deep sleep and relaxation.

The first step is to lie on your back or your side or simply be in your normal sleeping position. Put one of your hands on your forehead while the other on your stomach. Take note of your stomach climb up and down as you breathe.

Remain in this position for at least 10 minutes or as long as you like for the Reiki energy to flow. As you feel more relaxed, you will eventually fall asleep.

Reiki Exercise for Self-healing

This exercise makes use of meditation through the Reiki principles. It is intended for inviting good health, clarity and peace of mind, and curing illnesses.

The first step is to allow yourself to sit comfortably in an area where your feet are flat on the floor. You can also do a lotus or half-lotus position.

Next, cross both of your hands over your heart. You can also press your fingers and palms together in front of your heart.

Then, say these Reiki principles out loud: "Just for today (1) Do not be irate, (2) Do not be worried, (3) Be grateful (4) Work hard, and (5) Be kind to others.

And...the most important thing: smile and laugh, laugh and smile. It's free. Always has been and always will be!

Now, like I promised I will share with you certain Reiki tools I have developed as a part of my Reiki courses experiences (1-2 level). They will equip you with more healing strategies, plus, in case you are thinking of doing a Reiki attunement, you will feel more or less prepared. Again, this is something that I was taught and that I adjusted to my lifestyle and developed with personal practise.

You may think of it as a recipe book. Some people buy recipe books looking for specific recipes that they want to follow through. Some people get cookbooks as they are looking for inspiration, variety and flavours they can apply in their kitchen the way they want.

Both attitudes are awesome. It really depends on you and how you want your Reiki journey to be. If you find it easier just to follow though, then follow through. If you prefer to use my guidance as a template to create your own way, feel free to do so. Simply do whatever feels right for you now...

Reiki for quick self-healing: hands positions

After connecting to Reiki and purifying your energy field using Ken'Yoku, you may proceed to practising the following self-healing rituals. If you don't have time to go through the whole Ken'Yoku process from chapter 4, that's fine. Simply put the intention and do it quickly in your mind. Simply think that you want and need to connect to Reiki and be grateful for this amazing healing opportunity. You may also try to practise it on others, simply giving it a right intention.

Simply do what I do and observe your body, mind and spirit! Personally, I love the following self-healing techniques when I am in bed, ready to go to sleep, sometimes before an occasional nap, or first thing in the morning, when I am still in bed. It's kind of a prayer also!

Hands over your eyes

Hands over your jaw, thumbs under your ears

Hands on the back of your head, on your cranium, above the occipital bone

Both hands around your neck or on your throat balancing the throat chakra and unleashing unlimited creativity).

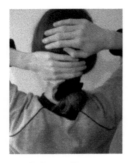

Left hand on your occipital bone and right hand above it.

Hands on your sternum (helps alleviate anxiety)

Right hand on your forehead, left hand on your occipital bone (great for creating new habits and getting rid of negative thoughts, emotions and also- addictions)

Both hands on the top of your head (making sure all your chakras remain balanced and staying mentally energized)

Chapter 7: Reiki Symbols and How to Use Them to Let Go of Past Situations, Create an Incredible Future and Attract Abundance

In this chapter, I am going share with your the three Reiki symbols that are usually studied during Reiki Level 2 course.

The symbols must be treated with respect and not abused. It means that you cannot use them to manipulate other people or selfishly feed your ego. The symbols will only work for you, if you use them for your highest good and also want to help others.

Different masters may have different procedures to go about using symbols. During my Reiki 2nd level course, we were asked to draw them using pen and paper, as well as drawing them in our imagination or in the air, with an incense stick.

It's okay if you are not a visual person. You may simply say them aloud, or, in your mind. Simply have the intention and they will help you increase the healing energy of your treatment.

You can even "draw" them in your mouth. Just imagine you are doing it with a tip of your tongue. It works great in emergency situations, for example headache, negative feelings, lack of energy...

CHO KU REI (my favorite symbol for some reason)

This is the first Reiki symbol. It brings the Universe to the Earth and helps transform celestial to physical. It can be employed in different situations, its main purpose being to intensify the healing energy.

For example, you have a headache and do a self-healing meditation; simply think of Cho Ku Rei and the healing energy of your treatment will be intensified. If you are working on someone else, visualize the symbol on their body or on the palms of your hands.

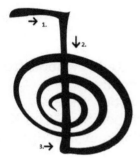

This symbol is especially recommended for physical ailments, all kinds of pain and sore muscles. If you are a massage therapist, you can use this symbol when working on your clients—the treatment will be intensified and made more holistic.

Cho-ku-rei is very often referred to as " The Power Simbol" or, "Light Enhancer."

Use Cho Ku Rei to attract abundance (I know that you have been waiting for this one for quite a few chapters now!):
-Connect to Reiki and enter a meditative state
-Write down all your financial wishes, make sure you make them positive (don't use negative language). For example, instead of saying: "I don't want to end up in debt," say, "I

deserve to live in abundance," or, "I choose to be offered a better job," or, "I attract amazing business opportunities and keep growing every day." You may also be specific and say, "I deserve to live in abundance and get paid at least (your chosen amount of income) per month or year," or, "I need to be wealthy in order to contribute more to this world." Put it the way you want, but remember it must be positive and ethical. You can't wish to get rich by stealing or lying.

According to Reiki principles, there is abundance for everybody, and one must be grateful for what they have.

Don't let greed turn you around. Using Reiki symbols from the point of greed will not do you any good.
-While you say your wishes aloud or in your mind, visualize, or call for the Cho Ku Rei symbol. Say, "Cho Ku Rei, I need your help and guidance." You may also draw it next to your wishes.
-Repeat this abundance meditation every day, at least twice a day. In order to expand your mindset, you may also turn the most important part into a mantra. Keep saying it while keeping your right hand on your forehead and your left hand near your occipital bowl. It will help re-program your mind and get rid of old, limiting beliefs.

You may also use this symbol to attract other amazing things. Simply write down your powerful affirmations and draw the symbol or say it aloud together with your affirmations. For example:

I deserve to be in a loving relationship.
I deserve to live a life full of passion.

I deserve to have a mission in life.
I deserve to expand my knowledge and do well in my
exams so that I can help the world.
I deserve to become a ...

-Use the Cho Ku Rei symbol to create endless affirmations to attract health, wellness, love and whatever it is that you wish to achieve—always for your highest good.

-Call upon this symbol to get rid of negative energies or when entering unknown spaces (for example a new house).

-Use it to protect yourself and your loved ones while traveling. My family lives on the other side of Europe, so I travel by plane quite a lot. Whenever on a plane (as well as other means of transportation), I recall Cho Ku Rei and ask it for a safe travel. Simply call upon it or visualize it entering the plane/train/bus/car. Have a nice and save journey and always be grateful when you reach your destination!

-Enhance the healing properties of foods and medications: again, simply put the intention, visualize or, if you are not a visual person, call Cho Ku Rei.

-Call it whenever feeling down and negative. Ask Cho Ku Rei for positive energy and emotional strength.

SEI HE KI

Are you ready for a total holistic body and mind transformation? I am sure you are – this is one of the reasons you got this book! We are now inviting the next Reiki symbol that is extremely useful in making all transformations easier, faster and more profound. This symbol stands for change; a positive change that elicits good situations.

SEI HE KI

-Sei He Ki is associated with light and the illumination. It helps get rid of emotional toxins and heals, especially on mental and emotional levels.

-It helps us discover the reasons for our failures as well as our bad behaviors and helps us become more self-aware and devise right solutions.

-When using this symbol, you may also add the previous symbol, Cho Ku Rei as it can intensify the effects of Sei He Ki.

-It acts upon both parts of the brain helping to achieve balance between creativity and science, eliciting peace and harmony. You know how people who are too scientific but lack the creative part may suffer, or the other way round when people who are too creative and always dream tend to miss the reality (again, this can lead to disappointments and frustration).

-It helps transform negative situations and behaviors into positive and empowering ones.

-It is best used as a healing addition to transformational

body, mind and spirit affirmations. For example, "I deserve to have unstoppable energy," or "I choose to eat healthy," or "I choose to eat foods that help me take care of my body and mind," or "I get up early with ease and passion."

-I especially recommend calling upon this symbol when you wish to break addictions and create new, powerful habits. Sei He Ki will help you make the transition easier.

HON SHA ZE SHO SHEN: Heal the past and create your future

HON SHA ZE SHO NEN

-This symbol goes beyond limitations of time and space.

-It goes beyond ego and rational thinking. It helps us reconcile with the past.

-You can evoke it in your mind, call it or draw it, when thinking about some past trauma, or a situation where someone treated you badly, or the other way round. Simply visualize the past situations you want to heal. You may even use a picture from those times (if you have one).

-You can use it to prepare yourself for future situations (stressful events, job interviews etc.). Create a powerful affirmation ("I will have an amazing time with my wife's family") and keep the symbol in front of you, draw it or say it aloud (or whisper it, or repeat in your mind).

-Many Reiki healers use this symbol to do a distance healing Reiki session. Even if you are not a professional healer, you may connect to Reiki and then send this symbol to someone you love. First ask the Universe. Say: *if the person X allows me to send them the healing energy, let it be so. If not, let the energy return to where it came from.*

Keep a picture of the person you wish to help in front of you.

Distance healing sessions are usually shorter and last anywhere from 10- 20 minutes.

To sum up, in this chapter, you have learned the first 3 Reiki symbols that can help you in your journey:

1. Cho Ku Rei- especially used for problems of physical and material nature (Don't forget to use it to attract wealth and abundance!)

2. Sei He Ki- especially used for problems of emotional and mental nature.

3. Hon Sha Ze Sho Nen- Especially used to help heal past traumas and also reduce anxiety, fear and uncertainty about future situations.

When you feel good, you attract a better life. Have you noticed how Reiki and Law of Attraction go hand in hand?

Chapter 8: Common Questions and Misconceptions about Reiki Explained

Due to the fact that Reiki's history has various versions, it is perhaps acceptable that many people misunderstood its real concept. Many people who develop a certain interest in this powerful healing method are tormented with curiosity as to what it truly is and how it works.

This chapter will discuss some of the most common questions and misconceptions about Reiki and clear them out as much as possible.

Is Reiki a religion?

We have talked about it before, but let's bring it up again…This is one of the most common questions about Reiki. The answer to this question is no, Reiki is not a religion; however, it is spiritual in nature. Reiki does not have a church, priests, liturgy, or sermons.

Reiki is based on principles, which are divulged to practitioners. These principles came from the Japanese Emperor whom Misao Ukui, the founder of Reiki, adored and honored.

At first I felt like some of my family and friends would disapprove of me writing this book, because they are Christian or Catholic and practising. However, I decided to have more trust in them as well as in myself. I knew that as soon as they see the reasons why I am doing what I am doing, they will not be sceptical anymore. I knew they would finally realize that I respect all the religions and those who practise them. After all, the Reiki principles are re-phrased Christian principles. It's all about becoming your best self and helping the world become a better place...

Is the Reiki practitioner the one healing the Reiki recipient?

This is a huge misconception about Reiki. The practitioner in Reiki can be likened to a garden hose that pours out the life force energy onto recipients in order for the latter to heal themselves. The practitioner serves as the facilitator of the recipient's healing. He or she channels the Reiki energy so the recipient can heal by himself/herself.

Does going through a single Reiki healing session mean an individual is healed for a lifetime?

Many people who have experienced Reiki healing wish that they can be healed forever. There may be a part of them that has changed and healed forever during a single Reiki session. However, Reiki healing is holistic. Therefore, it is a process and as such, it may take about three to four sessions (or more) to be healed totally depending on the individual's need to receive Reiki. The bottom line is, healing is a process that can also last a lifetime. View Reiki as a journey, not a quick, natural cure. There is always something new to learn and experience as you keep diving deeper and deeper into the Ocean of Reiki.

Do all practitioners give the same treatment?

The answer to this question is yes and no. Yes, because Reiki, both traditional and Western, are based on the same principles of healing. No, because not all Reiki practitioners make use of Reiki alone. Some integrate Reiki healing with other therapies.

Besides, everyone is different. It is advisable to choose a Reiki practitioner who has the adequate ability to channel energy and uses Reiki all the time. Listen to your gut – choose a practitioner/healer whose energy you find most appealing.

If an individual decides to become a Reiki practitioner, will he/she never get sick?

It should be clear to anyone who is interested in becoming a practitioner that Reiki Masters and practitioners are human and not divine. Simply stated, they are mere mortals. They also go through problems and negativities like other people do. Regardless of if they are on an advanced spiritual level, Reiki Masters and practitioners are still human, and are therefore not perfect and can get sick.

The only difference is that they have natural tools to stimulate healing faster and more effectively. Besides, the regular practise of Reiki and embracing a healthy, natural lifestyle and personal development helps fight stress and create a positive mindset that are also natural cures when it comes to fighting disease.

We should also not forget that Reiki practitioners, thanks to a regular Reiki practise, are able to prevent many imbalances. Ever since I practised Reiki, I get sick much,

much less. <u>But I can't say I never get sick</u>. However, if I do, I usually fight it faster. I used to be really prone to colds and flu, and I still may get something in the winter.

These sicknesses typically last only a couple of days instead of a couple of weeks. I must also admit that my lack of illness is due to other natural therapies I practise (yoga, alkaline diet, aromatherapy, phytotherapy and positive thinking). Reiki forms a part of a healthy, balanced lifestyle and is enhanced by a healthy nutrition and proper self-care.

My blog holisticwelnessproject.com is my personal "holistic lifestyle" platform where I share the best and the most effective natural therapies and personal development techniques that I myself utilize on a regular basis. Check it out!

In order to become a Reiki practitioner, should I actually pay for the course? Or should these be free? What is the best way to go about it?

This is a really good question and I personally have heard different opinions on it. To be honest, I am in the middle of the road with the answer.

You see, some Reiki advocates say that Reiki treatments, courses and attunements should always be free so that everyone can enjoy them, while others say that in this materialistic world, whatever becomes free can lose its value.

In my opinion, they are both right in a way. You see, the actual Reiki treatment is free and will always be. This is something that we all have inside, plus the universal energy is free. However, oftentimes in order to get re-connected to the universal energy, we need someone to prepare us and make sure we can be energy channels so as to help others and ourselves. Here's the thing, if a person who helps us with the attunement process, is a professional healer and they do it full-time, why should we expect their time and dedication for free?

Imagine you go to see your hairdresser and expect a free haircut. Of course, if your friend is a hairdresser, they may offer you a free haircut or a "services swap." It depends on both of you. I paid what seems to me now a really symbolic amount of money both for my Reiki 1 and Reiki 2 course. It was money well-spent. I invested in it myself.

Now I can heal myself and others! I personally have never charged for a Reiki treatments just because I don't see myself as a professional healer and I have other sources of income.

The reason why I wanted to learn Reiki was mainly for my own spiritual journey and personal development, plus I wanted to become a Reiki practitioner so as to combine it with massage treatments.

But, at this stage of my life, I am more focused on coaching and writing as well as creating courses, so Reiki is a tool that I use to remain focused and energized. If a friend of mine asked me for a Reiki session, I would do it for free. I would also do it for free for a stranger, but again, if I had to do it every day, or on a more regular basis, I would need to charge for my time.

If I were to concentrate on Reiki as my main way to contribute to the world, I would thus reject my other activities that help me make a living. I would need to charge so as to pay my rent and buy food, right?

Again, follow your intuition. Some places offer free Reiki attunements, and some practitioners may also be volunteers. There is also nothing wrong with paying for one, as long as you know it will benefit you and you will actually make a good health investment down the road.

Paying for a Reiki treatment or a course will not detract from their healing energy, as long as you and your Master have the right attitude and the intention. It's as simple as that.

I want to receive Reiki from an experienced practitioner. But how do I find one? How do I know they can help me? Does the healing world also have scammers and charlatans?

The best way to find one is via mouth-to-mouth advice. I recommend that you try to find some of the patients he or she has treated and talk to them.

However, as long as you can call them or even visit them in their work place (whether it is a studio, a private apartment- may healers work from home, a spa- nowadays many holistic spas offer Reiki treatments, or a retreat center), you can always talk to them personally, tell them what your problem is and simply listen to your gut. Do you like them? Do you want them to work on you?

I have booked a session with a Reiki practitioner. Is there anything I need to do before I attend it?

A good practitioner will either send you all the information by e-mail or explain to you by phone, so that you are prepared. Usually, you will be asked to wear comfortable clothes, take off your shoes as well as jewellery, glasses and contact lenses (in some cases). Some professional Reiki healers will send you a questionnaire you can comfortably fill in at home, before the session. This may help if your problem is something you feel a bit ashamed of discussing. You simply put it on paper so that they are better prepared to help you.

Other than that, they may ask for past diseases, treatments, traumas and other natural therapies you are using. A good Reiki healer will prepare you for the session. If you see they are not motivated to do so (which hardly ever happens, most people in this "sector" are extremely passionate about what they do), simply don't let them work on you.

They say that the Universal energy is always the same, no matter who uses it and that we should rid ourselves of judgment (something I agree with), but if you feel like you don't connect with your healer, simply search for another one.

It's important to get on well, as oftentimes you will be telling them about your problems.

Is it true that some people cry during Reiki and Reiki initiation process?

Yes, it's truth, and I have seen it many times. But this is nothing to worry about. If you cry to purify your energy field and let the old pain and traumas go, then it's good for you. These are normal reactions. It may happen to you as well, but you will feel relieved. So...have no fear!

A friend of mine who completed her Reiki 1 attunement really enjoyed it, but after that she got sick for a week and felt emotionally shattered. Why? Shouldn't Reiki make you feel good? I now think I am scared of Reiki and don't feel like giving it a shot...

After the initiation process, as well as after continuing your Reiki journey with second and third level Reiki courses, you will be getting rid of old mental and emotional toxins. Something in your friend was stuck there and was preventing her from achieving real personal success and happiness.

Crying and feeling sad or emotionally imbalanced is just a temporary state that occurs as a part of a healing process. Just like people who do cleanses and detoxes, they may feel bad only to feel an incredible energy after a couple of days.

So again, have no fear. Be ready to get rid of the old, so that you can start again. Remember that everyone deserves another chance to be happy!

Whenever I do my Reiki meditation, I pray for you and all my readers. Even though we haven't met before, we are all connected. Isn't it great to know that there is someone out there, on the other side of the globe, praying for you? Knowing that, how can you possibly afford to feel sad?

Conclusion: Embrace Reiki and Feel Amazing Like You Have Always Wanted!

Congratulations for reading this book until the very last page. I hope you enjoyed it as much as I enjoyed every second of writing it for you. Use it as a coffee for your soul whenever you feel to nourish yourself in a holistic way!

Be sure to sign-up for my Mindfulness Newsletter to receive your free bonus resources:

www.holisticwellnessproject.com/mindfulness

It will help you keep on "holistic track", and amplify what you have learned from this book.

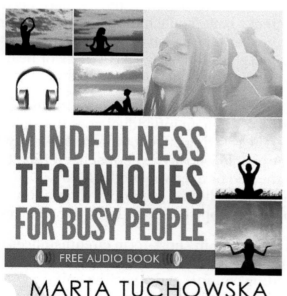

Problems with your sign-up? Let me know:

info@holisticwellnessproject.com

I am here to help!

Let's sum up what we have talked about during our Reiki journey:

-The Reiki System has many variations; however, in essence, its treatments help the individual physically, mentally, emotionally, and spiritually. It is an art of healing that is open to anyone regardless of age, gender, race, or religion;

-Reiki may have different effects on each individual who receives or experiences it, which depends on their needs. Some people may or may not feel anything during a Reiki session. However, most individuals who have experienced Reiki report the system's benefits including deep relaxation and a sense of calmness and peace on all levels of their well-being. Others feel sensations such as tingling or heat while some feel that their inner energies were restored;

-Reiki is intended not only for physical healing. It can also be a soothing treatment when an individual goes through tough times in life. The relaxing effect of the Reiki energy can be beneficial for people who are experiencing difficult times or feel disconnected or overwhelmed. Reiki treatments can bring the feeling of peace as well as allow an individual to focus and cope better with life's challenges;

-Although Reiki is beneficial in short-term circumstances, it can also aid an individual in dealing with long-term conditions by providing comfort and a positive mindset. Generally, when an individual observes positive changes taking place in his/her life, it is advisable to continue with the Reiki therapy or sessions;

Before you go...I need your help! If you enjoyed reading this book, could you please rank it on Amazon and post a short review? I am always happy to receive feedback and encouragement from my readers. It's you I am writing for and I want to provide as much value as I possibly can. Your review will help me create more inspirational books for you and your loved ones. Whenever I get a review, it puts me in a positive state and I read all of them every single day! Thanks in advance!

Finally, I would love to keep in touch with you for years to come!

Let's connect via my blog and social media:

www.HolisticWellnessProject.com

More Books by Marta Tuchowska

(Available on Amazon-Kindle, Paperback and Audible Formats)

Learn more at:

www.HolisticWellnessProject.com/spirituality-books

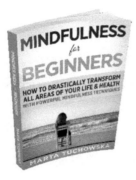

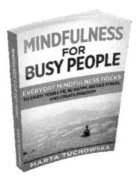

Lightning Source UK Ltd.
Milton Keynes UK
UKHW022024131120
373373UK00003B/524